Invigorate Your Church

By
Archie Parrish

SERVE INTERNATIONAL • ATLANTA, GEORGIA

Invigorate Your Church

Published by Serve International, Inc.
4646 North Shallowford Rd., Suite 200
Atlanta, GA 30338

First printing, 2001
Printed in the United States of America
ISBN 1-930976-02-X

Dedication

This book is dedicated to two church leaders: in the *Church Militant, Harry Reeder and in the *Church Triumphant, Robert Fraley.

Harry Reeder is senior pastor-teacher-leader of the Briarwood Presbyterian Church, Birmingham, Alabama. For more than twenty years, Harry's passion for revitalizing churches has inspired thousands of leaders across denominational lines. One of the highlights of my life has been to work with him developing the conference ministry of *Embers to a Flame.*

Robert Fraley was a committed Christian, devoted husband, godly friend, successful businessman, the founder and president of Leadership Enterprises, Inc. Robert served with me on the Board of Directors of Ligonier Ministries for nine years. God promoted him from the Church Militant to the Church Triumphant October 25, 1999.

* The Church exists in two modes: the Church Triumphant composed of all saints now in heaven; the Church Militant composed of all believers still on earth. The militant church maintains its vitality by use of a holy rhythm. On the Lord's Day, guided by gifted leaders and workers, it gathers for strength through nurture: worship, teaching, equipping, learning, and fellowship. Throughout the week the saints scatter to faithfully continue Christ's mission through work, mercy, service, witness, and evangelism.

Table of Contents

Acknowledgements

This book is the product of more than forty years of ministry; therefore, it is impossible for me to properly acknowledge all who contributed to its development. When I became a Christian, God gave me a hunger for His Word. I began carrying a small Bible and reading it whenever I had the opportunity. Dr. Charles Seidenspinner, President of Southeastern Bible College, Birmingham, Alabama, was one of my first mentors. I can still see him leading the student body singing, "I love Thy Church, O God." He taught me that God is not so much interested in mere evangelism as He is in building His Church to the glory of His name. Dr. "S" once told me I would never be poor if I poured my fortune into my heart and head. He believed that reading a good book was spending time with the author. He developed in me an appetite for reading that is still growing as I grow older. Throughout this book, you will see numerous titles and authors. This is an attempt to give credit where credit is due; however, I know I have left out many.

Al LaCour, pastor of ChristChurch, Atlanta is my present pastor. His passion for grace, sonship, and Christian community has provided opportunity for me to live out in Christian community many of the truths described in this book.

I owe special acknowledgement to four coworkers at Mission to North America, of the Presbyterian Church in America. Jim Bland, Coordinator of Mission to North America, has consistently encouraged me in the developing of the Kingdom Campaign. Off and on for almost thirty years, I have mentored Jim. Now it is my delight to work under his leadership. Tim McKeown, Multicultural Coordinator, has enriched the content of this book on the multiethnic nature of the Church. Ron Shaw, Director of Spiritual Life/Mission to the World, provided insight on missionaries and how to effectively pray for them. Dave Peterson, Coordinator for Chaplain's Ministries, has provided direction on how to pray for military chaplains.

I also want to acknowledge many pastors who have been my coworkers in developing and implementing the Kingdom Campaign: Al Baker, Golden Isles Presbyterian Church, Saint Simon's Island, GA; Bill Barton, St. Andrews Presbyterian Church, Columbia, SC; Steve Jennings, Westminster Presbyterian Church, Jacksonville, FL; Steven Beck, Grace Church, Toronto, Canada; Dan King, First Presbyterian Church, Stanley, NC; Gary Cox, Briarwood Presbyterian Church, Birmingham, AL; Dan Perrin, Faith Presbyterian Church, Cincinnati, OH; Lee Ferguson, Covenant Presbyterian Church, Columbia, SC; Jim Wright, Heritage Presbyterian Church, West Columbia, SC; Patrick Womack, Carolina Presbyterian Church, Locust, NC; Mike Ross, Trinity Presbyterian Church, Jackson, MS; Wilson Benton, Kirk of the Hills Presbyterian Church, St Louis, MO; Tim Witmer, Crossroads Community Church, Upper Darby, PA; Ray Ortland, Jr., First Presbyterian Church, Augusta, GA; Lee Capper, Faith Presbyterian Church, Cumberland, MD; Jim Phillis, Covenant Presbyterian Church, Hendersonville, NC; David Eby, North City Presbyterian Church, Poway, CA; John Ragland, Hope Presbyterian Church, Atlanta, GA; R. C. Sproul, St. Andrews Chapel, Lake Mary, FL; Brad Evans, Presbyterian Church of Coventry, Coventry, CT; David Schutter, Foothills Community Church, Sturgis, SD; Doug

Griffith, Carriage Lane Presbyterian Church, Atlanta, GA; Bill Thompson, Metro North Presbyterian Church, Goose Creek, SC; Dan Kiehl, Covenant Presbyterian Church, Glen Mills, PA; Dale Welden, Covenant Presbyterian Church, Fayetteville, GA; Rod Whited, Pinewood Presbyterian Church, Middleburg, FL, John Kinser, Covenant Presbyterian Church, Milledgeville, GA; Scott Puckett, University Presbyterian Church, Orlando, FL; Tom Henry, Christ Covenant Presbyterian Church, Matthews, NC.

Finally, I must express my deep gratitude to Genny Collins, my administrative assistant who has meticulously read, reread, and corrected this manuscript. And Gary Hitzfeld, Director of Ministry for Serve International, my coworker and friend, whose insights have added much to this book and even more to my personal growth in Christ.

Before You Begin

This book does not try to present a comprehensive doctrine of the church (ecclesiology); it concentrates on the militant church as God's army. Nor does this book try to present a general manual of church renewal; rather, it attempts to show the strategic value of praying with kingdom focus for the leaders and workers of your church so that it becomes all God desires it to be as seen in God regularly adding new believers to it and its participation in planting new congregations.

The material included here is to be used for stage three of The Kingdom Campaign,[1] a movement aimed at building a super-critical mass composed of 120 kingdom intercessors in 120 local churches in 120 metro areas in North America. The objective of The Kingdom Campaign is twofold: to equip believers to develop the daily discipline of kingdom-focused prayer and to encourage them to multiply after their kind, that is, to train others to do the same.

Invigorate Your Church seeks to build on the process that was begun in *Improve Your Prayer Life* and continued in *Intercede For and With Your Family*. If you worked

---

[1] If you have not read the free sixteen-page booklet, *The Kingdom Campaign* (available from Serve International, 4646 N. Shallowford Rd., Suite 200, Atlanta, GA 30338), please do so now. It comes with *Improve Your Prayer Life* and describes the best process for learning the material in this book and implementing a supercritical mass of kingdom-focused prayer in your local church. It will explain the foundations upon which *The Kingdom Campaign* is built, and will also show the role of the other books in *The Kingdom Campaign* series: ***Improve Your Pray Life, Intercede For and With Your Family; Invigorate Your Church; Impact Your World;*** and ***Ignite Your Leadership*** (Leader's Guide for the four stages).

through these two manuals, you should already be praying daily with a kingdom focus for 30 minutes. In this book, you will be encouraged to add another 15 minutes to that time—for a total of 45 minutes daily. To do that, you will need to plan time to work through the material in this book as well as to plan time each day to pray. Be sure to read the introductory remarks of the Discussion Guide (pages 155 through 156) before you begin reading the text on page 19! You will find directions there for working through the text and for continuing to develop the daily discipline of kingdom-focused prayer.

Always Something More!

To celebrate my 65th birthday, Anne, my oldest daughter insisted that I go parasailing in the Florida Keys. Heights and I do not usually mix with comfort but since Anne arranged for our whole family to enter into the celebration, I went along with the idea. Cy, my grandson, was the first to fly. Then Phylis and Amanda, my daughter-in-law and granddaughter, went up. When they returned to the deck of the boat, Amanda pleaded to go up alone. She was too small and too young. She turned to me and said, "Granddad, you are going up, aren't you?" I would have gone up if it killed me rather than disappoint her. So they strapped on the harness and reeled out the 600 feet of line. For thirteen years, I lived in South Florida, and I had seen this stretch of land under a variety of circumstances, including tropical storms and hurricanes. But as I rose to an altitude of about 500 feet, I saw beauty I had never seen before and my fear of heights was transformed into awe! I saw the blue Atlantic below me and to the west was the Gulf of Mexico. There were schools of fish, frolicking dolphins, and it was sooo quiet. The only sound was the wind moving past my ears. Spontaneously I burst out singing:

> "O Lord my God when I in awesome wonder
> Consider all the works Thy hands have made,
> I see the stars; I hear the rolling thunder,
> Thy power throughout the universe displayed.
>
> "When through the woods and forest glades I wander,
> And hear the birds sing sweetly in the trees,
> When I look down from lofty mountain grandeur,
> And hear the brook and feel the gentle breeze.
>
> "Then sings my soul, my Savior God to Thee;
> How great Thou art, how great Thou art."[2]

In my thirteen years of living in South Florida, I had seen this piece of land many times. But hanging from a parachute 500 feet above the water I saw so much more than I had ever seen before.

What is true of God's material creation is also true of His spiritual creation, the Church. There are two ways of viewing the church—from earth and from heaven. The church in history is one thing. The church in eternity is quite another. The heavenly church is always so much more than the earthly church. Positionally believers now "*sit together in heavenly places in Christ Jesus*."[3] But actually we are still in this world.[4] Even if the earthly Church were always at its best, it would not begin to compare with the

---

[2] Carl Boberg written about 1885. Manna Music, Burbank, CA, 1955.

[3] Ephesians 2:6

[4] See John 17:18

HEAVENLY CHURCH! Scripture declares that the world has nothing but sinners in it.[5] The church is composed of people God calls out of the world. These called out sinners are at various points in the process of being conformed to the image of Christ.[6] The process of being conformed to the image of Christ will not be complete until God glorifies His people.[7]

The church in history is a counter culture to the fallen world. When the church conforms to the world it becomes a subculture and people are attracted to it more for personal gain than for God's glory. Then the church becomes a mixed multitude of believers and unbelievers. History shows that some people have sought to use the church to satisfy their own egotistical ambitions. There are times when the actual church has been more a synagogue of Satan[8] than the bride of Christ.[9] The Crusades and the Inquisition are devilish blots on the reputation of the institutional church. And hardly a week passes that spiritual conflict does not result in splitting both local churches and denominations. Under persecution, only those who are serious about their faith will identify with the church. The church is at her best when the world is at its worst, when standing for Jesus will probably mean dying for Him.

The church from a heavenly, eternal perspective is "*a glorious church, not having spot or wrinkle or any such thing, but ... holy and without blemish*."[10] Whenever we try

---

[5] See Ecclesiastes 7:20; Romans 1:28-2:1; 3:9, 19; 11:32; Galatians 3:22; 1 John 1:8-10

[6] See 2 Corinthians 3:18

[7] See Romans 8:29-30

[8] See Revelation 2:9; 3:9

[9] See Ephesians 5:25-32

[10] Ephesians 5:27

to describe *this Church,* we quickly realize that whatever we say, *this Church* is always something more! The eternal church is constantly invading time and space transforming the earthly more and more into the heavenly so that we are increasingly aware that the church on earth is more than what meets the eye. The earthly church is an institution. In fact, it is the largest institution in the history of the world. But it is more than an institution; it is a community, but it is more than a community. It is an army, but it is more than an army. The Church is a business. God requires the church to submit itself to human laws in so far as these laws do not contradict the laws of God. The government requires churches to keep basic records and function within business guidelines, etc. Thus the Church is a business, but it is more than a business. The Church is an organization, but it is more than an organization. It is an organism—like a body.

Because of the discrepancy between the present incomplete, imperfect church and the future complete and perfect church, many people reject the whole church, and to use a cliché, they throw out the baby with the bathwater. Satan cheers this error on by trying to convince those who act in this manner that they are not as hypocritical as the imperfect people who still participate in imperfect churches. But Scripture makes it abundantly clear that Christians cannot become what God desires them to be apart from active regular participation in the specific local church in which God has prepared them to minister. For believers to be vital, they must be connected in a vital local body in a "giving and receiving" relationship.

Paul has the Church in mind when he prays that the Ephesians "*may be able to comprehend with all the saints what is the breadth and length and height and depth.*"[11] Paul Minear says it well, "To comprehend the magnitude of the church requires divine power and wisdom, because the church's existence is a visible token of the mystery of redemption. Since this mystery is spoken of several times as of the glory of God, it is perhaps safe to suppose that the dimensions of Christian community are derived from the dimensions of God's glory. This community's horizons are ultimately as far-flung as the range of divine glory."[12]

---

[11] Ephesians 3:14-19

[12] Paul Minear, *Horizons of Christian Community,* St. Louis, MO: Bethany Press, 1959, p. 26.

A Church Deceived

"Satan himself transforms himself into an angel of light," declared Paul; therefore, he feared that as *"the serpent deceived Eve by his craftiness,"* so the minds of the Corinthian church might be corrupted from the simplicity that is in Christ.[13] If Paul were with us today, he would express this same concern for the American evangelical Church, which in its desire to be relevant and successful has become selectively worldly. Howard Snyder expresses,

> Evangelical churches protest the world's values at some points (sexual morality, family life, abortion) but have been seduced by the world at others (materialism; personal and institutionalized self-interest; styles of leadership, motivation and organization; the uses of power). Many Christians are convinced that technology changes things, even if they are unsure that prayer does. Technology works better than grace in the technological society.
>
> Perhaps it is true that what's good for General Motors is good for the church. But at what price? Certainly the church can powerfully use the ways of the world. But is it then still the church of *God's* kingdom? Take a Madison Avenue approach, and you get a Madison Avenue Church.[14]

---

[13] See 2 Corinthians 11:2, 3, 13-15.

[14] Howard A Snyder, *Liberating the Church,* Intervarsity Press, Downers Grove, IL 1983, p. 14.

To a great degree, the American Church in its passion for worldly success has departed from *"the simplicity that is in Christ."* Consequently, it does not function as a militant army engaged in spiritual combat. Rather it is more like a corporation engaged in competitive peacetime business.

Early in His public ministry, Jesus warned the religious leaders, *"Do not make My Father's house a house of merchandise!"*[15] Again only hours from the cross, *"Jesus went into the temple and began to drive out those who bought and sold in the temple, and overturned the tables of the money changers and the seats of those who sold doves. And He would not allow anyone to carry wares through the temple. Then He taught, saying to them, 'is it not written, "My house shall be called a house of prayer for all nations"? But you have made it a "den of thieves."'*[16]

The Church is not a peacetime business but a wartime army. God's purpose for the church as the army of Christ is to witness by its very existence to the victory that He has won and is winning over the devil. And this witness is to both a watching world *and* to the principalities and powers in the heavenly places. Thus God's army has a double assignment expressed by the Apostle Paul in these words:

> *I was chosen to explain to everyone this plan that God, the Creator of all things, had kept secret from the beginning. God's purpose was to show his wisdom in all its rich variety to all the rulers and authorities in the heavenly realms. They will see this when Jews and Gentiles are joined together in his church. This was his plan from all eternity,*

---

[15] John 2:16

[16] Mark 11:15-17

> *and it has now been carried out through Christ Jesus our Lord.*[17]

As Paul viewed the matter, the Church is to be the one people of God (Jews and Gentiles joined together) faithfully continuing Christ's mission at the same time to mankind and to principalities and powers. The two arenas cannot be separated because men's wisdom and loyalties are the primary battleground on which the conflict rages.[18] Therefore, let us pray with the apostle Paul, "*May He be given glory in the church and in Christ Jesus forever and ever through endless ages. Amen.*"[19]

---

[17] Ephesians 3:8-11 NLT

[18] Minear, *Horizons of Christian Community,* p. 55.

[19] Ephesians 3:21 NLB

What is the Church?

Charlie scornfully challenged, "When your church is perfect, like the church in the Acts of the Apostles, I will join it." I was serving as pastor of three small congregations in rural North Alabama. Charlie was the neighborhood "hard case."

"Charlie, what is it about the church that you don't like?" I asked.

"Marie is a member of your church, isn't she?

"Yes," I responded.

Charlie continued, "I've known Marie for over twenty years. Six months ago, she said she became a Christian and you baptized her. Now she's a member of your church. Yesterday she was in my store buying groceries. Some of the price tags were wrong so she accused me of trying to cheat her. She lost her temper. If she's a good Christian, I'm an astronaut. And believe me, she's not the only hypocrite in that church."

"Charlie, you said you've known Marie for more than twenty years. Have you noticed anything different about her in the past six months?"

"Well, I have to admit her language is much cleaner and she doesn't blow up as often as she used to, but she's a long way from being a *good Christian*!"

"Charlie," I asked, "Are you perfect?"

Angrily he fired back, "We're not talking about me! I've never claimed to be perfect, but I believe people that say they are Christians ought to be perfect."

"Charlie, I've got some bad news and some good news for you. The bad news is this: if our church were perfect (which, by the way, the church in the Acts of the Apostles was not) and you joined it, it would no longer be perfect. "The good news is that the church in this world is not perfect because *no one* in the church is perfect—and we won't be perfect in this lifetime. When I became a Christian, I learned a poem. It goes like this:

'I am not what once I was,
Nor am I what I want to be.
But what I am, I am by grace,
And when I meet Him face to face,
I will be like Him perfectly.
I once was dead, yet thought I lived,
And now I live, yet dead I am.
I live in Him in Whom I died.
I to the world am crucified.
My life my song is Calvary's Lamb.'[20]

"Marie is not what she wants to be, she certainly is not what she will be, but she is definitely not what she used to be! I can't excuse Marie loosing her temper any more than I can overlook my own sin. But you need to understand that while becoming a Christian is something that happens at a point in time, it is preceded by one process and it is followed by another process. In the Bible becoming a Christian is called being "*born again.*"[21] When you were born physically you were conceived and your mother carried you in her womb for nine months. Then you were born and from that moment to this day, you've been growing. That's the way it is with spiritual life. God's Spirit takes His Word and gives life to our dead souls, and then we trust Christ and are "born again." After this, God's

---

[20] Vance Havner, *Hearts Aflame,* Fleming H. Revell, Westword, NJ, 1952, p. 100.

[21] See John 3:3, 5

Spirit continues to use His Word to enable us to grow. Marie is still a spiritual infant. She's not perfect, but she is forgiven and she is growing.

"All genuine members of the church are like Marie. The Church in this world is not a museum in which God displays perfect specimens. No, the church is more like a field hospital in a combat zone. I served with the 1st Marine Division in the Chosen Reservoir Campaign during the Korean War. The temperature at times was twenty degrees below zero Fahrenheit and the enemy out numbered us a least ten-to-one. Almost fifty percent of our troops were killed or wounded. In this hostile situation, doctors and medical corpsmen suffering from frostbite, pneumonia, and flesh wounds, treated marines who had the more severe battle wounds. We all had problems but we worked together and we survived."

"Charlie, the Lord takes us as we are—not merely wounded by sin but "*dead in trespasses*."[22] Then He gives life to our sin-deadened souls, and starts the process of making us like His Son, Jesus."

Charlie's desire for the perfect church is widely shared today. More than 80 percent of the adults who get counted as new adherents are really just transplants from other churches. Barna calls them, "religious consumers in search of the perfect, or at least more exciting or enjoyable, church experience." Barna continues, "Disturbingly little church growth is attributable to new converts. All in all, it was not a good decade for church growth." In spite of the nation's population increase and climate of rising interest in spirituality, Christian churches actually decreased in size

---

[22] Ephesians 2:5

during the '90s. They went from an average of 99 adults attending on an average Sunday in 1990 to 90 adults present on a Sunday in 2000. The reasons for the shrinkage include the opening of several thousand new churches (which often start out with fewer people than the average existing church has); an increase in the number of unchurched adults; and the decreased frequency of attendance among church goers. Claims of prolific church growth have been grossly exaggerated, not only are most churches not increasing in size, but those that are expanding are doing so at the expense of other churches."[23]

My conversation with Charlie was in reality a spiritual battle, and it had a number of outcomes. To my knowledge Charlie never became a Christian. Marie continued to grow in her spiritual life: her two sons came to faith in Christ, her husband recommitted himself to Christ, and they established family worship as a regular part of their life.

The encounter with Charlie prompted me to dig deeper into the subject of the Church. Jesus declared, "*I will build My church, and the gates of Hades shall not prevail against it.*"[24] Notice Jesus did not say, "I will build your church," and He certainly did not say, "You will build My church." In the first century, the Jews, the heathen and the followers of Jesus had significantly different perceptions of the church.

First Century Perceptions

The Jews: For a while the Jews called the Way a sect (Acts 24:14). A sect is a group of people who take one tenant of

---

[23] George Barna and Mark Hatch, *Boiling Point, It Only Takes One Degree,* Regal Books, Ventura, CA, 2001, pp. 235-236.

[24] Matthew 16:18

belief and emphasize it in a disproportionate manner over the whole system of belief. In addition to the Way, the Jews also termed the followers of Christ as Galileans (Acts 2:7) and Nazarenes (Acts 24:5).

The Heathen: Luke tells us, "The disciples were first called Christians in Antioch" (Acts 11:26). As herodians belonged to Herod and were followers of Herod (Matthew 22:16), so Christians belonged to Jesus and were followers of Christ. The name was evidently given to the followers of Christ by the Gentiles to distinguish them from the Jews. Jews would not call Jesus' followers Christians. Unbelieving Jews used the word *Christos* to refer to the Messiah, and they did not believe Jesus was the Messiah. The three uses of Christian in the New Testament are from the heathen standpoint: here in Acts 11:26, then in Acts 26:28 (a term of contempt in the mouth of Agrippa), and finally 1 Peter 4:16 (persecution from the Roman government). It is a clear distinction from both Jews and Gentiles and it is not strange that it came into use first here in Antioch when the large Greek church gave occasion for it.

Christians as a Third Race-- The vast majority of ancient authors persisted in regarding Christians as an utter abomination and charged them with, "Hatred of the empire and emperor, and uselessness from the economic standpoint." Christians were held responsible for any great calamity that occurred. [25]

Tertullian, in his *Apology* and in his address *ad Nationes,* seeks to refute the charge brought against Christianity, of

---

[25] See "Christians as a Third Race, in the Judgment of Their Opponents," Adolph Harnack, *The Mission and Expansion of Christianity in the First Three Centuries,* Gloucester, MA, 1972, pp. 266-278.

being something exceptional and utterly inhuman. Tertullian agreed that Christians "Are indeed called the third race of men…on the score of religion and not of nationality … the Romans first, then the Jews, and after that the Christians." Harnack concludes: "Third race" was a common designation for Christians on the lips of the heathen in Carthage about the year 200. And this designation referred exclusively to the Christian method of conceiving and worshipping God. After the middle of the third century, both empire and emperor learned to recognize and dread the third race of worshippers as a "nation," as well as a race. They were a state within a state. In reality, this "Third race", this "nation" was composed of people of every race and every nation.

The followers of Christ: The first followers of Christ called themselves disciples (learners), believers, brethren, saints, and those of the Way. Jesus called himself "the Way", the only way to the Father (John 14:6). This term "Way" has its roots in the Jewish definition of life as in Isaiah 40:3 "the way of the Lord," Psalm 1:6 "the way of the righteous," "the way of the wicked." In the Acts of the Apostles, Luke frequently describes Christianity as the Way (See Acts 9:2; 16:17; 18:25; 19:9, 23; 22:4; 24:22). From Paul's letter to the Ephesians we receive great insight into the nature of the Church.

Ephesus

Before considering Paul's letter, let us look at the city of Ephesus. Ephesus was the third largest city in the Roman Empire. Historians and archaeologists place the peak population during the second century at between 200,000 and 600,000. Only Rome and Alexandria had more residents. Ephesus was called the first and greatest metropolis of Asia and the cradle of Hellenistic civilization. Ephesus was a beautiful city of amazing art and architecture. The Temple of Diana was considered one of the Seven Wonders of the World.[26]

Ephesus has been called a nursery and garden of Christianity, the second province of God after Jerusalem. Cosmopolitan Ephesus was the best starting point for the church's universal character and mission. "There were all races and colors of God's creatures that made up the international character of Ephesus. They did not all come back to their respective countries, but those who did took with them the news about the new hope and the Gospel of the living God."[27]

Ephesus later was named *Ayasoluk*, which is a popular abbreviation of the Greek, *Haghios Theologos*, meaning the Divine Theologian and it proudly bore this name for some

---

[26] John T. Wood, an English architect, started his long search for the Temple of Diana in 1963 and finally found its ruins on December 31, 1969. Excavators found that the temple has passed through five phases of construction (the earliest beginning about 600 B.C.) and the edifice Paul and John would have known was begun about 350B.C. and destroyed by the Goths during the third century invasion. The temple itself was 180 feet wide and 377 feet long. 117 sixty-foot columns supported the roof. These columns were six feet in diameter and thirty-six of them were sculpted at the base with life size figures. The temple stood on a platform 239 feet wide by 418 feet long. The holy of holies was apparently open to the sky and contained an altar twenty feet square, behind which the statue of Artemis stood. Artemis or Diana was equated with the Asia Minor Cybele, the mother goddess. As worshipped in Ephesus, the goddess was a very orientalized fertility deity. Her statue was a many-breasted figure. "Ephesus," *The Biblical World, A Dictionary of Biblical Archaeology,* Ed. Charles F. Pfeiffer, Baker Books, Grand Rapids, MI, pp. 229-230.

[27] Marko Zuzic, *A Short History of St. John in Ephesus,* The American Society of Ephesus, Lima, OH, 1960, p. 29.

fourteen centuries in memory of the beloved Disciple of Jesus. At the end of World War I, the Turkish Government changed the name to *Selcuk* honoring the first Moslem conquerors who incorporated Ephesus into the Moslem world at the end of the 14th century.[28]

The Ephesian Church

Paul preached the gospel in Ephesus "*for two years, so that all who dwelt in Asia heard the word of the Lord Jesus, both Jews and Greeks*."[29] The Ephesian Church was not a like a modern large downtown church. Rather it consisted of numerous house churches scattered across the city and throughout the province of Asia Minor. Paul planted this church.[30] Later he sent Timothy to strengthen it,[31] and still later through John in exile on the Isle of Patmos, the glorified Christ wrote to the church of Ephesus. Christ commended them for their hard work, perseverance, morality, and doctrinal orthodoxy. Yet in spite of these commendable points, Jesus said, "*I have this against you, that you have left your first love." He warned them to repent and return to the first works, or else, "I will come to you quickly and remove your lampstand from its place*."[32]

When the aged Apostle John returned from his exile on the Isle of Patmos, he had a major power confrontation, a spiritual showdown with the worshippers of Diana in her temple. Ramsey Mac Mullen, Dunham Professor of Classics and History at Yale University, accepts as valid

---

[28] Marko Zuzic, *A Short History of St. John in Ephesus,* The American Society of Ephesus, Lima, OH, 1960, p. 11.

[29] Acts 19:10

[30] See Acts 18:19 ff

[31] See 1 Timothy 1:3ff

[32] Revelation 2: 1-7

history the account that John entered the Temple of Diana or Artemis and prayed, "O God…at whose name every idol takes flight and every demon and unclean power: now let the demon that is here take flight at Thy name…" The record reports that while John was saying this, all of a sudden the altar of Artemis split in many pieces…and half the temple fell down. Then the assembled Ephesians cried out, "There is but one God, the God of John!… We are converted, now that we have seen Thy marvelous works! Have mercy on us, O God, according to Thy will, and save us from our great error!"[33] And the people of Ephesus turned from Artemis to Jesus. Within the next fifty years this cult almost ceased to exist and the Ephesian Church became the center of world Christianity.

When John died, tradition claims he was buried on the hillside overlooking Ephesus where he wrote his Gospel. His mausoleum became a church. Eventually the Basilica of St. John was built. When the hearts of the Ephesian believers burned hot with "first love" for Jesus, the gospel spread throughout the ancient world. But when this "first love" cooled, the hard working, orthodox Ephesian believers, degenerated into monument builders. Over a period of about 300 years, they built the Basilica of St. John on a scale that rivaled the Temple of Diana. It was the first major place of worship built by Christians and was the sixth largest church in the world, after St. Peter's Basilica in Rome, the Cathedral in Florence, Sacred Heart in Brussels, the Cathedral in Reims, and the Cathedral in Cologne. This shrine concept of the church was a radical departure from the apostle's Paul's teaching to the church he planted in this city.

---

[33] Ramsey Mac Mullen, *Christianizing the Roman Empire, AD 100 to 400,* Yale University Press, New Haven, CT, 1984, pp. 25ff.

Charles Van Engen summarizes Paul's thinking on the Church as found in his epistle to the Ephesians.

> The word church (*ekklesia*) appears only nine times. This is surprising when we consider that Ephesians is usually regarded as expressing the height of Paul's view of the Church. The absence of the word *ekklesia*, then, should make us aware that Paul is here developing his thought with Hebrew-style pictorial representation or images, rather than with Greek logical propositions. A closer look reveals that at least fifteen different word pictures are employed. The most important of these are saints (used nine times), body (used eight times), soldier with armor (used eight times), and wife (used seven times). A series of lesser images embellish the major conceptions: chosen people of God (used four times), sons or family (used four times), workmanship, building, or temple (used three times), a song of praise or offering (used two times), new man, or new self (used two times). Finally a whole range of images flash once: the breadth, length and depth of love; imitators of God, kingdom of Christ, children of light, wise men, and ambassadors.[34]

Paul's concept of the Church as Christ's Body[35] embraces all believers of all time in all places. Each local or particular church is a complete "body," a microcosm of the whole church. It is in relation to "the body" that the term "member" appears. Members are not the 'club' type but the

---

[34] Charles Van Engen, *God's Missionary People, Rethinking the Purpose of the Local Church,* Baker Book House, Grand Rapids, MI, 1991, p. 49.

[35] See Ephesians 1:23; 3:6; 4:4; 4:16; 5:30; See also 1 Cor. 12:12, 13, 18-20, 31.

'body' type. 'Club type membership' usually begins with the desire of the individual to join a club then a membership committee selects candidates based on pedigree, social position, wealth, etc. Usually club members pay an initiation fee and then use the facility as they desire—usually for personal benefit. In 'body membership' all members are interdependent under the control of their head. All members must be connected, both giving and receiving.[36]

The final metaphor, the one to which all the others point and build, is the church as an 'army.' Says Paul,

> *Finally, my brethren, be strong in the Lord and in the power of His might. Put on the whole armor of God, that you may be able to stand against the wiles of the devil. For we do not wrestle against flesh and blood, but against principalities, against powers, against the rulers of the darkness of this age, against spiritual hosts of wickedness in the heavenly places. Therefore take up the whole armor of God, that you may be able to withstand in the evil day, and having done all, to stand. Stand therefore, having girded your waist with truth, having put on the breastplate of righteousness, and having shod your feet with the preparation of the gospel of peace; above all, taking the shield of faith with which you will be able to quench all the fiery darts of the wicked one. And take the helmet of salvation, and the sword of the Spirit, which is the word of God; praying always with all prayer and supplication in the Spirit, being watchful to this end with all*

---

[36] See "Membership," C. S. Lewis, *The Weight of Glory, and Other Addresses,* Macmillian, New York, 1980, pp. 106-120.

> *perseverance and supplication for all the saints--and for me, that utterance may be given to me, that I may open my mouth boldly to make known the mystery of the gospel, for which I am an ambassador in chains; that in it I may speak boldly, as I ought to speak.* [37]

Frequently, this passage is misread. Paul is not giving moralistic advice to individual Christians to improve their character. In reality, he issues a military command to the Christian community and to individuals only as members of the army of Christ. On the church as God's army of fighters against Satan, Paul Minear comments,

> Throughout the New Testament the Kingdom of God was understood in antithesis to its enemy, the kingdom of Satan. The two kingdoms embraced the only possibilities confronting men. The beginning of the new kingdom was traced to the victory by Christ over Satan. This victory was accessible to all who would enlist in the same battle and would use the same weapons. The community, therefore, thought of itself as a company of soldiers, fighters against Satan. Their existence was bounded by the course of the dramatic and victorious struggle. Wherever the kingdom of God came, there this warfare was joined. "*If I cast out demons with the finger of God, surely the kingdom of God has come upon you.*"[38] Between the two kingdoms there could be no compromise or appeasement. The power of God's kingdom forced man to a radical and final

---

[37] Ephesians 6:10-20

[38] Luke 11:20

choice between two armies and their commanders. It was obvious that Christ's soldiers must use the weapons that he provided. To don those weapons was precisely the same as to "put on" the new man and "put off" the old.[39]

This understanding of life in the context of celestial struggle was rooted in the Genesis story of the Fall, as the episode had been interpreted by apocalyptical seers. Satan had been present and active in the Garden in the form of the tempting and accusing serpent. The same foe had asserted his power in the wilderness of temptation and in the Gethsemane struggle, as well as in every decisive work of the new Adam. To follow this new leader required constant and recurring participation by the band of disciples in the same temptations and offenses. At the inception of one kingdom, Satan had succeeded by deceit in establishing his reign of sin and death; at the inception of the other kingdom, Christ had succeeded in replacing the order of deception and futility with the order of truth and life. The two kingdoms, therefore, had similar beginnings, but they were as disparate as the treachery and the faithfulness of the men who represented two humanities.[40]

---

[39] See Ephesians 4:24

[40] Minear, *Horizons of Christian Community*, pp. 120-121. For a fuller development of this picture of the army, see also R. Leivestad, *Christ the Conqueror* (The Macmillan Co.- 1954), pp. 272-285.

An Army Engaged in Spiritual Combat

The Apostle Paul sees the Church as a wartime army engaged in spiritual combat. To the Corinthian church he declared, "*Thus I fight: not as one who beats the air. But I discipline my body and bring it into subjection, lest, when I have preached to others, I myself should become disqualified*[41] and "*though we walk in the flesh, we do not war according to the flesh. For the weapons of our warfare are not carnal but mighty in God for pulling down strongholds, casting down arguments and every high thing that exalts itself against the knowledge of God, bringing every thought into captivity to the obedience of Christ, and being ready to punish all disobedience when your obedience is fulfilled.*"[42] Furthermore, Paul pleaded with the Roman believers, "*Now I beg you, brethren, through the Lord Jesus Christ, and through the love of the Spirit, that you strive together with me in prayers to God for me.*"[43] And Paul encouraged the Colossian Christians with these words: "*Epaphras, who is one of you, a bondservant of Christ, greets you, always laboring (fighting) fervently for you in prayers, that you may stand perfect and complete in all the will of God.*"[44] To Timothy he exhorted, "*This charge I commit to you, son Timothy, according to the prophecies previously made concerning you, that by them you may wage a good warfare.*"[45] "*Fight the good fight of faith.*"[46] "*You therefore, must endure hardship as a good soldier of Jesus Christ. No one engaged in warfare*

---

41 1 Corinthians 9:26-27

42 2 Corinthians 10:3-6

43 Romans 15:30

44 Colossians 4:12

45 1 Timothy 1:18

46 1 Timothy 6:12

entangles himself with the affairs of this life, that he may please him who enlisted him as a soldier."[47] And as Paul anticipated the close of his life and ministry, he wrote, "I *have fought the good fight, I have finished the race, I have kept the faith.*"[48] Can there be any doubt that the Apostle Paul saw the Church as a wartime army engaged in cosmic spiritual combat?

John Bunyon takes many of the Bible's thoughts on this subject and pictures them in his classic allegory *The Holy War.*[49] In this work Bunyon describes how Lucifer devised the strategy to transform the castle of Mansoul from a garrison for men of war into a warehouse for goods. All was paradise in Mansoul until the day that the wicked prince Diabolos determined that he must have this city for his own. Lucifer devised a most effective strategy. He explained to his demonic horde, "Mr. Sweet-World and Mr. Present-Good are men that are civil and cunning, but they are our true friends and helpers. Let those be engaged in this *business* for us, and let Mansoul be taken in much *business*, and if possible with much pleasure and this is the way we will overthrow them. Let us but cumber and occupy and amuse Mansoul sufficiently, and they will make their castle a warehouse for goods instead of a garrison for men of war."

This diabolical advice was highly applauded throughout hell till all the lesser demons, while obeying their orders, gnashed their teeth with envy and malice at Lucifer for having thought of this masterpiece and for having had it

---

[47] 2 Timothy 2:3-4

[48] 2 Timothy 4:7

[49] John Bunyon, *The Holy War,* Moody Press, This work is available in many editions. Wilbur Smith's work is complete with introduction and index.

received with such loud praise.[50] Lucifer's strategy was and still is most effective. Many churches today are indeed so taken in much *business* and much *pleasure* that they have been overthrown. They are cumbered and occupied and amused. They have made *their castle a warehouse for goods instead of a garrison for men of war*.

In the New Testament the idea of conflict stands close to that of faith. Conflict is a comprehensive term for wrestling with the inner and outer assaults on the existence and witness of the Christian—a wrestling that has to be militant and that carries with it effort, danger, and distress. The foes are principalities, powers, rulers of the darkness of this age, spiritual hosts of wickedness in the heavenly places. And though our foes are not flesh and blood, the context of Paul's command implies that some of the most significant battles will be fought in our key human relationships; as husbands or wives, as parents or children, as employers or employees.

The early church saw itself as the army of Christ. Leon Podles observes, "The western use of the term *sacramentum* to describe the liturgical actions of the Church carries military overtones. The *sacramentum* was the oath sworn by the soldier inducted into the army, and it transformed his life. He put aside civilian concerns and henceforth devoted his life to military affairs. Civilians were dismissed in soldier's slang as *pagoni,* hicks, and Christians took over the term to describe those who had not enlisted in the army of Christ. Such use of military terminology emphasized the agonic nature of the Christian life, the struggle with Satan and all the forces of evil. The

---

[50] Alexander Whyte, Bunyon Characters of the Holy War, Oliphant, Anderson and Ferrier, London, 1902, pp. 131-132.

soldier has always been a potent image of the self-sacrificing Savior."[51]

Leon Podles also reminds us that Christian baptism is a rite of initiation. "Christianity is based upon a story of sufferings, followed by resurrection, redemption, and accent into a better life that is an uncanny parallel of the narrative enacted in almost all ritual initiations."[52] In baptism a Christian puts on Christ; the believer dies and is reborn with Christ. With Christ the believer descends into the abyss, confronts death—indeed dies—and is reborn to a new life.[53] The Christian who is most fully conformed to that death and resurrection is the best imitator of Christ; the martyr therefore most clearly fulfills the Christian call.[54] All Christians, both men and women, are called to be athletes of Christ, soldiers against Satan, and to act in a militant manner in the spiritual realm. In the Early Church, the baptismal creed had a threefold affirmation of the Trinity and a corresponding threefold rejection of the world, the flesh, and the devil.[55]

Early Christians believed that liturgy should possess a quality the Hebrews called *kavod* (glory) and the Romans *gravitas* (gravity); both words at the root mean 'weightiness' and connote a sense of dignified importance and seriousness.[56] While the Church in Scripture is the

---

[51] Leon, J. Podles, *The Church Impotent, The Feminization of Christianity,* Spence Publishing, Dallas, TX, 1999. p. 88.

[52] David Thomas, *Not Guilty: The Case in Defense of Men* (New York: William Marrow, p. 57.

[53] (Podles, *The Church Impotent, The Feminization of Christianity, p.* 88).

[54] Ibid., 89.

[55] Ibid., 91.

[56] Patrick M. Arnold, *Wilderness, Warriors, and Kings: Masculine Spirituality in the Bible (Crossroad: New York, 1991) p. 77.* Quoted in Leon, J. Podles, *The*

bride of Jehovah and the Lamb,[57] The individuals who make up the Church are called to be imitators of the Son in His sacrifice. Both men and women should participate in this spiritual militancy.[58]

Luther certainly concurred in this understanding of the Church. He rejected most of the comforting medieval devotions to saintly intercessors, mediators, and protectors, and returned to a stark view of humanity caught between God and the devil. Marc Leinhard observes:

> The evocation of the devil by Luther is something more than a simple medieval heritage. If he spoke of the devil so often (and more deeply than was done in the Middle Ages), it is because he understood the whole of world history as a battle of demonic power against God the Creator and Redeemer. Evil is not simply moral or a weakness of people, but transpersonal, bound to that mysterious power which Luther called, with the tradition, Satan or devil.[59]

Thus believers are never at rest, but are in incessant combat against the world, the flesh, and the devil.

Church Impotent, The Feminization of Christianity, Spence Publishing, Dallas, TX, 1999, p. 151.

57 See Revelation 19:7; 21:9; 22:17

58 Podles, *The Church Impotent, The Feminization of Christianity, p,* 86.

59 Marc Leinhard. "Luther and the Beginnings of the Reformation," in *Christian Spirituality: High Middle Ages and the Reformation, ed.* Jill Raitt, (New York: Crossroad, 1987), p. 293. Quoted in Leon, J. Podles, *The Church Impotent, The Feminization of Christianity,* Spence Publishing, Dallas, TX, 1999, p. 87.

Sons are soldiers! The begetting of the Son by the Father and the begetting of the Christian by God is a revelation of something humanity could never have imagined. The Son is truly begotten of God; he is not simply "like" God, the closest thing to God of any creature; rather he is the same substance (*ousia*) as God. He is the only-begotten; there is no other like him.[60]

Yet Christians are also begotten in a sense that surpasses all metaphor and is almost impossible for reason to fathom. The Son, pouring forth the Holy Spirit, creates other sons. He conforms both men and women to his own image as the Son, by making them all God's sons. …Christians are the children of God, growing into the image of the Son, that they may also become sons of the Father.[61]

In essay after essay, Danish philosopher, Soren Kierkegaard contrasts the smooth, bland, effortless, comfortable Christianity of his country with the poverty, persecution, rejection, and martyrdom of those who seriously follow the way of true Christianity. Said Kierkegaard, "Verily there is that which is more contrary to Christianity . . . than all heresies and all schisms combined and that is to play Christianity. But precisely in the very same sense that the child plays soldier, it is playing Christianity to take away the danger . . . and in place of this to introduce power (to be a danger to others), worldly goods, advantages, luxurious enjoyment." He uses the word leniency to describe the "common Christianity in the land" and exclaims: "When one sees what it is to be a Christian in Denmark, how could it occur to anyone that this is what Jesus Christ talks about: cross agony and suffering,

---

60 Podles, *The Church Impotent, The Feminization of Christianity,* p. 87.

61 Ibid.

crucifying the flesh, suffering for the doctrine, being salt, being sacrificed, etc.? No, in Protestantism, especially in Denmark, Christianity marches to a different melody, to the tune of 'Merrily we roll along, roll along, roll along'--Christianity is enjoyment of life, tranquillized."[62]

Verily there is that which is more contrary to Christianity . . . than all heresies and all schisms combined and that is to play Christianity.

Kierkegaard's comments are as applicable to most American churches today as they were to the churches of Denmark in his day. But to be honest, few American churches today are even *playing* war. Consciously or unconsciously, most American churches are functioning in a peacetime business mode. Pastors are CEOs, the chief executive officers; the staff's role is to manage with the goal of being the biggest and the best, maintaining the organization or just surviving. Their elders or deacons are the board of directors. Some "CEOs" are so obsessed with beating their competitors that they become egotistical sheep-stealing empire builders. Success is measured by the crowds attracted and the efficient management of the organization. Those seeking the survival or maintenance of their organizations are defensive, too cautious and self-centered. When the church is seen as a peacetime business there is little prayer and much of the prayer that does exist is shallow, self-centered, sentimental, and unbiblical. Members are consuming customers. Political activism replaces Gospel proclamation, prayer and fasting. Sister

---

[62] Dean Kelley, *Why Conservative Churches are Growing, A Study in Sociology of Religion*, Harper & Row, New York, 1972. pp. 120-121. Also see "Life Is War," pp. 19-31 and "War In the Bible," pp. 33-67, *Improve Your Prayer Life, by* Archie Parrish, Serve International, Atlanta, GA.

evangelical churches are seen as competitors rather than comrades in arms. Hired staff replaces gift-based lay ministry. Finances rather than bold faith determines expansion.

American Churches: A Business Enterprise

The most objective sign that a church is not a wartime army is the way it uses money. American evangelical churches, on average, spend 96% of all their monies in North America, the vast majority of these dollars are spent on themselves, especially new buildings. Of the remaining 4%, local and global evangelism receives 3.5% and the unreached peoples of the earth receive the last .5%.[63] The "edifice complex"--obsession with buildings and the activities that go on in them--causes many churches to borrow large amounts of money to finance immense, elaborate structures. Some then find themselves with a severe shortage of resources for ministry. Sometimes the annual debt service on borrowed money exceeds the church's missions giving. Too often this indebtedness leads to disproportionate time spent in fund raising and the use of techniques that generate funds but are questionable from a biblical point of view; preferential treatment for the wealthy, selection of officers more for financial net worth than spiritual qualification. Efficient management methods become substitutes for biblical disciplines such as prayer and fasting. In some cases ministries become such well-oiled machines that they can be "successful"--judging from the numbers--even without the Holy Spirit.

---

[63] These numbers are supported by Dr. Larry D. Ressor, Founder and President of Global Focus; P.O. Box 2428; Woodstock, GA 30188.

Hans Domizlaff, German advertising man, was asked to help the failing church in his homeland to attract worshippers. In his reply to the churchmen, he said:

> If you (reverend sirs) are not able to find the way back to an unconditional self-criticism . . . which will make possible a new beginning, no advertising techniques in the world will be able to stop the end from coming. If God has forsaken you, what advice can we poor advertising men give you? Men will not stop seeking God, but they will choose other mediators. Do you no longer understand, reverend sirs, what it was that actually gave that little group of apostles on the day of Pentecost such tremendous power that it was sufficient to transform the face of the Western world? These were not advertising media in the ordinary sense; it was rather the influencing power of faith, an unshakable faith in the mission of Christ and the redemption in life and death, which accomplished the miracle. Because you yourselves no longer feel the influencing power of faith within you, you try to substitute tactical cleverness for the missing suggestive aid of a strong soul. And when you do that you sink ever deeper into the realm of no response.[64]

The church is not a peacetime business needing only efficient management, the church is a wartime army engaged in spiritual combat. To be a victorious army, the church, both leaders and workers, must respond to God's call to be His people and to faithfully continue Christ's mission on earth.

---

64 *Hans Domizlaff, advertising man* (Quoted in Helmut Thielicke's. *The Trouble with the Church,* Harper & Row, New York, 1965, p. xiii)

God's Call to be His People

The Church is not a volunteer human organization, like a social or civic club. The Church is a divine organism in which only those who are called by God can participate. Paul explains that God "*has saved us and called us with a holy calling, not according to our works, but according to His own purpose and grace which was given to us in Christ Jesus before time began.*"[65] Saving us means that God makes His name ours by making us His. Through the prophet Isaiah the Lord commanded, "*Bring My sons from afar, and My daughters from the ends of the earth--everyone who is called by My name, whom I have created for My glory; I have formed him, yes, I have made him.*"[66] Christ promises, "*The one who comes to Me I will by no means cast out.*"[67] The Lord who calls you by His own name also calls you by your name: "*Fear not, for I have redeemed you; I have called you by your name; you are Mine.*"[68] He calls you individually but not alone.

Edmund Clowney comments, "The calling of the kingdom is the power of God that brings us from darkness into light and sets us as lights in the darkness. To seek first the kingdom of God means to seek first the purpose of God's saving rule in Christ. Seeking the kingdom is not a pious attitude that can link with any activity whatever. It is selective, restrictive, focused action. Paul likens it to military service. The soldier on service may not become involved in other pursuits; he is under orders.[69] Seeking the

---

[65] 2 Timothy 1:9

[66] Isaiah 43:6-7

[67] John 6:37

[68] Isaiah 43:1

[69] See 2 Timothy 2:4

kingdom contrasts with seeking the objectives of the world: food, clothing, shelter.[70] Our heavenly Father knows our needs and will supply them, but building bigger barns to store surplus crops for our own ease and security is not seeking the kingdom of God; it is worldly folly, the service of mammon.[71]

"The distinction commonly made between secular pursuits and Christian service comes dangerously close to the distinction between what the Gentiles seek and what the children of the kingdom seek. Christian calling cannot be secular. The man who hesitates between a moneymaking career and the ministry is not merely in doubt about his calling to the pastorate; he is questioning his commitment to Christ."[72]

All whom God calls to trust Christ, He also calls to be members of Christ's body.

All whom God calls to trust Christ, He also calls to be members of Christ's body. Paul explains, "*God has set the members, each one of them, in the body just as He pleased*."[73] How do Christians determine in which local church they are supposed to be a member? Should they select a church based on the eloquence of the preacher, or the youth programs, or the music ministry, or the largest building? Paul would say none of the above is adequate reason to join a church. God uniquely gifts each member to provide particular ministry in a particular church.[74] "*For*

---

[70] See Matthew 6:25-34

[71] See Luke 12:13-21

[72] Edmund Clowney, *Called to the Ministry,* Inter-Varsity Press, Chicago, IL, 1964, p. 20.

[73] 1 Corinthians 12:18

[74] See 1 Corinthians 12:11

we are His workmanship, created in Christ Jesus for good works, which God prepared beforehand that we should walk in them."[75] Therefore, we should determine what our spiritual gifts are and where these gifts can be best used for the "*edification of the church*."[76] When this is done, some believers will be leaders and others will be workers in various ministries—but none will be without some gift designed to help the local church be the people of God and faithfully continue Christ's mission on earth.

God Calls Leaders to Lead

All whom God calls to salvation He also calls to serve. Some He calls to lead. When Paul planted churches, he prayerfully appointed elders, and he instructed Titus to do likewise.[77] In God's economy, leaders are essential for the church accomplishing Christ's mission. God does not choose leaders as the world does. The Apostle Paul said to the Corinthian believers, "*Simply consider your own calling, brothers; not many of you were wise, humanly speaking, not many mighty, not many noble. But God has chosen the world's foolish things to put to shame the learned; and God has chosen the weak in the world to shame the strong. God has chosen the world's insignificant and despised people and nobodies in order to bring to nothing those who amount to something, so that nobody may boast in the presence of the Lord*" (1 Cor. 1:26-29 Berkely). Being wise, mighty, or noble does not automatically mean that one is qualified to lead the people of God. The history of the Church reveals that few geniuses or rulers were humble enough to be used as leaders of

---

[75] Ephesians 2:10

[76] 1 Corinthians 14:12

[77] See Acts 14:23; Titus 1:5

God's people. It is to those who recognize themselves as "nobodies" that God gives the passion, the gifts and the call to be leaders.

Godly character is essential for leaders. The apostle Paul describes the virtues necessary for leaders of Christ's church.[78] More than 400 years before the birth of Jesus, Sun Tzu, a Chinese General and philosopher said that war must be appraised in terms of five fundamental factors, the first of which is moral influence. By moral influence Sun Tzu meant that which causes the people to believe in their leaders, so that they will accompany them in life and unto death without fear of mortal peril. Chang Yu, another Chinese General said "When one treats people with benevolence, justice, and righteousness, and reposes confidence in them, the army will be happy to serve their leaders.[79] The Church's Commander-in-Chief is the Lamb that has been slain. He never calls His followers to go anywhere He has not first gone or do anything that He has not first done.[80] Eugene Petterson sees this element of moral leadership in the teaching of Jesus. In *The Message* he translates Matthew 7:29 "It was apparent that he was living everything he was saying—quite a contrast to their religion teachers! This was the best teaching they had ever heard."

Intellectual and moral authority are important, but divine authority is not limited to our finite understanding and our

---

[78] See 1 Timothy 3; Titus 1:6-9

[79] Sun Tzu, *The Art of War*, Translated and with an Introduction by Samuel B. Griffith with a forward by B. H. Liddell Hart, Oxford University Press, New York, 1963 PP. 63-64. This work is among the greatest classics of military literature ever written. Much of it can be applied with great value to spiritual warfare.

[80] See John 10:4

ability to do all that we know we should do. Sinful humans, even when redeemed, are not perfect. Divine authority is God's delegated glory and not to use it or to misuse it is treason.

Church leaders, especially pastors, should be their congregations' chief prayer warriors. Effective church ministry begins with the pastor's personal prayer life; it moves to his family and then embraces his ministry to his flock and his world. As the God-appointed leader of the flock, the pastor sets the pace and the pattern for the whole congregation.

Jesus Christ is the pastor's model in all things--especially prayer. Jesus was exceptionally busy, often having no time even for meals. But he did not sacrifice his prayer time. The demands upon Him became a call to devote extra time to prayer.[81] Jesus Christ, by His example, has taught us the duty of prayer. However, He did not pray merely to set us an example: prayer was one of those things that was necessary for Him in order that He might "*fulfill all righteousness*."[82] But example, as set by Him, is the very strongest. If in such a life as His there was not only room but also need for prayer, much more must there be room and need in such lives as ours.[83]

As pastors follow Christ's example in the practice of prayer they become good examples for their flocks.[84] Paul

---

[81] See Mark 6:31; Mark 1:32-35; Luke 5:15-16; John 6:15

[82] Matthew 3:15

[83] Alfred Plumber, *Commentary on the Gospel of Luke* T & T Clark, Edinburgh, 1960, p. 391.

[84] It is impossible to stress too strongly the place of example in the ministry of the Gospel. Jonathan Edwards emphasizes the role of example in the Great Awakening (Archie Parrish, *The Spirit of Revival,* Crossway, 2000, p. 69-72.

exhorted two pastors to be examples for the members of their flocks.[85] When a congregation is on a spiritual plateau or declining, the impact of the pastor's prayer life is essential for bringing new vitality to it. George Barna observes, "A turnaround church is resuscitated partly due to the wide-spread and heartfelt prayer that is lifted to God on the church's behalf. The pastor emerged as a true prayer giant, taking hours and hours every week to beseech God for all that was needed in the turnaround experience."[86] Leaders should continuously pray, "Father, help me to be Your son and equip my flock to most effectively improve their prayer lives, intercede for and with their families, invigorate their church and impact their world for Your kingdom and Your glory."

Prayer is essential to balance the visible and the invisible dimensions of life and ministry. Without prayer, leaders and their followers become prey for the world, the flesh, and the devil. E. M. Bounds reminds us, "Air is not more necessary to the lungs than prayer to the preacher. The preacher must pray and the preacher must be prayed for.[87]

Believers are called to be the people of God so that they can faithfully continue Christ's mission on earth. From the

---

Also check Willis Peter De Boer, *The Imitation of Paul, An Exegetical Study,* J. H. Kok, N. V. Kampen, Amsterdam, 1962. Barnabas Lindars, "Imitation of God and Imitation of Christ, Duty and Discrimination," *Theology Vol. 76,* 1973, pp. 394-402. D. M. Stanley, "Become Imitators of Me": the Pauline Conception of Apostolic Tradition. E. J. Tinsley, "Some Principles for Reconstructing a Doctrine of the Imitation of Christ, *Scottish Journal of Theology*, pp. 45-57. E. J. Tinsley, *The Imitation of God in Christ, An Essay on the Biblical Basis of Christian Spirituality,* SCM Press Ltd., London, 1960.)

85 See 1 Timothy 4:12; Titus 2:6-8

86 George Barna, *Turn-Around Churches*, Regal Books, Ventura, CA, 1993, p. 52.

87 E. M. Bounds, *The Complete Works of E. M. Bounds on Prayer* (Grand Rapids, MI: Baker Book House, 1990), p. 486.

New Testament Church we learn that it is *not* the church that has a mission, but the very reverse: the mission of Christ creates His church. Mission does not come from the church; it is from mission and in the light of mission that the church has to be understood.[88] It has been accurately observed, "The Church exists by mission as fire exists by burning."[89] For churches to accomplish Christ's mission on earth they must have vigorous workers.

God Calls Workers to Work

The church is a charismatic community, which means God gives *every believer* spiritual gifts. Furthermore, He expects these gifts to be used to enable the church to be His people and faithfully continue Christ's mission.

Human community is the kingdom community *only* when it is formed around Jesus and lives by the Spirit for the sake of the Kingdom.[90] Where two or three come together in Jesus' name, there is potential for the 'church.' The New Testament church is a community of people called by Jesus, gathered around Jesus, committed to Jesus, worshiping Jesus and serving Jesus in His Kingdom in the world. Believers gathered round Jesus is the irreducible minimum of the church.[91] Dietrich Bonhoeffer explains, "Because Christian community is founded solely on Jesus Christ, it is a spiritual and not a psychic reality. In this it

---

[88] Jurgen Moltmann, *The Church in the Power of the Spirit A Contribution to Messianic Ecclesiology*, Harper & Row, New York, Copyright 1977, p. 10.

[89] Quoted by Charles Van Engen, *God's Missionary People, Rethinking the Purpose of the Local Church,* Baker Book House, Grand Rapids, MI, 1991, p. 27.

[90] Howard Snyder, *The Community of the King,* InterVarsity Press, Downers Grove, 1976 , p. 128.

[91] Ibid., 116.

differs from all other communities. The Scriptures call 'pneumatic,' 'spiritual,' that which is created only by the Holy Spirit, who puts Jesus Christ into our hearts as Lord and Savior."[92] Thus Christian community is not something believers work up; it is a gift from God that believers must appropriate. And prayer is a primary means for experiencing Christian community.

The New Testament church is a community of people called by Jesus, gathered around Jesus, committed to Jesus, worshiping Jesus and serving Jesus in His Kingdom in the world.

One very significant thing about Jesus' three years with his disciples is not just the miracles and the teaching and the crowds, but *the embryonic community that Jesus himself formed.* Jesus Himself provided for the many converts of Pentecost by preparing a community of disciples--not a disconnected corps of experts. How different from today's missionary and evangelistic methods which are more closely related to Madison Avenue than Scripture.[93]

Paul declares that the Christian community is a holy temple in the Lord. The teaching of the apostles and prophets is its foundation. God fits believers into this community stone by stone; Christ Jesus is the cornerstone that holds all the parts together.[94] Peter adds that the stones are "living stones" -- people whose dead hearts have been brought to life by the work of the Holy Spirit and the house that is built is

---

[92] Dietrich Bonhoeffer, *Life Together,* Harper & Brothers, New York, 1954. p. 64.

[93] Snyder, *The Community of the King,* pp. 117-118.

[94] See Ephesians 2:15-22

spiritual.[95] My pastor, Al LaCour, explained to our congregation, "Each member of the local church – young or old, male or female, educated or uneducated, rich or poor– is viewed as a living stone in a cathedral for Christ's praise and presence. Brick buildings require that each block be cast from the same mold to fit together smoothly. But, in a 'living stone' cathedral, each person is unique. God is building us into a living community with Christ as the Master Builder."

Christian community starts at the point of commitment and covenant. There is no genuine Christian community without a covenant, whether this covenant is formal or informal. Christian community cannot exist without commitment to Jesus as Lord and to each other as God's people. This must be more than a general mental ascent; it must be specific and explicit, involving our time, energy and resources. Covenant is not just a nebulous pledge to each other; it takes specific shape in history.[96]

Christian community cannot exist without commitment to Jesus as Lord and to each other as God's people.

The early church took shape primarily in the homes of the believers. Its life was nourished in homes in two ways. First, the church built through normal family life, drawing on the strength of the family in that day. Second, it was fed through *koinonia* groups, cells of people who met together for prayer, worship and the Eucharist who passed on Jesus' teaching by word of mouth. Normal family life in the

---

95 See 1 Peter 2:4-5

96 Snyder, *The Community of the King,* p. 127. See also Elton Trueblood, *The Company of the Committed, A Bold and Imaginative Re-thinking of the Strategy of the Church in Contemporary Life,* Harper & Row, New York, NY, 1961.

devout Jewish home included intensive and extensive training in prayer.[97] Prayer that pleases God is not the mere expression of the instinct possessed by all human beings made in God's image. Nor is it mere traditional form. Prayer that pleases the Lord is the Spirit-enabled, reverent cry of God's adopted sons seeking God's glory by persistently asking their Father for their promised inheritance.[98] This is Kingdom-focused prayer, prayer as our Lord taught us to pray.

The Lord's Prayer. Luke tells us "*Now it came to pass, as He was praying in a certain place, when He ceased, that one of His disciples said to Him, 'Lord, teach us to pray, as John also taught his disciples.'* "[99] The unnamed disciple appeals to the example of John the Baptist. At the time of Jesus, prayer customs and forms marked individual religious groups. This was true of the Pharisees, the Essenes, and as we perceive from this text, the disciples of John as well. A particular prayer expressed the particular relationship with God, which bound the group together. Joachim Jeremias paraphrases the request in this way; "Teach us to pray as men should pray who are already partakers of the coming reign of God."[100] In other words, the disciple asked for a prayer that would keep him and the other disciples focused on Christ's mission. The Lord's Prayer is the divinely inspired mission statement of the followers of Jesus. When this prayer is properly prayed it both expresses and appropriates Christian community.

---

97 See Joachim Jeremias, *The Prayers of Jesus,* Fortress Press, 1967, Philadelphia, PA, pp. 72-75.

98 See Romans 8:15, 26; Galatians 4:5; Matthew 6:9-13; Luke 11:1-4

99 Luke 11:1

100 Joachim Jeremias, *The Prayers of Jesus,* pp. 77, 94.

Christian community also provides a base for offensive spiritual warfare. Martin Luther expressed it this way, "The Kingdom is to be in the midst of your enemies. And he who will not suffer this does not want to be of the Kingdom of Christ, he wants to be among friends, to sit among roses and lilies, not with the bad people but the devout people. O you blasphemers and betrayers of Christ! If Christ had done what you are doing who would ever have been spared?" [101]

The Lord's Prayer is the divinely inspired mission statement of the followers of Jesus.

The Holy Spirit gives gifts to members and then sets "*each one of them, in the body just as He pleased.*"[102] The importance of members knowing and using their spiritual gifts is illustrated by the following parable:

> A group of animals decided to improve their general welfare by starting a school. The curriculum included swimming, running, climbing and flying. The duck, an excellent swimmer, was deficient in other areas, so he majored in climbing, running and flying, much to the detriment of his swimming. The rabbit, a superior runner, was forced to spend so much of his time in other classes that he soon lost much of his famed speed. The squirrel, who had been rated "A" as a climber dropped to a "C" because his instructors spent hours trying to teach him to swim and fly. And the eagle was disciplined for soaring to the treetop when he had been told to

---

[101] Bonhoeffer, *Life Together,* p. 64.

[102] 1 Corinthians 12:18

> learn to climb, even though flying was most natural for him.[103]

The church is not an animal farm filled with dumb beasts trying to do something God never expected them to do. Each person's special God-given gifts contribute to the Body. My pastor, Al LaCour, expressed it this way, "The Bible lists both 'ordinary' and 'extraordinary' spiritual gifts. Sincere Christians have disagreed on the nature of the 'sign and wonder' gifts after the time of the Apostles.[104] It is important to say that *some gifts* are confirming signs to *reveal* Jesus Christ to the world, in His Person and written Word. But all gifts are given to enable His Body to reflect Him to the world. Jesus becomes real to the world when His praise and presence are embodied in a community of gifted, loving believers who serve others in His Name. Therefore, your gifts, whether public or private, up-front or behind the scenes[105], are indispensable to help complete a picture of Jesus Christ to our world today."

Four prerequisites for discovering your spiritual gifts are: 1. You must be a real Christian. God only gives spiritual gifts to members of the Body of Christ.[106] 2. You must believe that God gives spiritual gifts.[107] 3. You must be ready to work and use your gifts, reflecting God's workmanship in your life.[108] 4. You must pray for wisdom in using your God-given gifts. James, the brother of our Lord urges, "*If any of you lacks wisdom, he should ask God, who gives*

---

[103] Charles Swindoll, quoted in *Daily Bread*, Radio Bible Class, Grand Rapids, MI, September 1, 1976.

[104] See 2 Corinthians 12:12

[105] See 1 Corinthians 12:20-25

[106] See 1 Corinthians 12:4-7

[107] See Hebrews 2:4

[108] See Ephesians 2:10

generously to all without finding fault, and it will be given to him. [109]

Three benefits of knowing and using your spiritual gifts are: 1. You will be a more effective Christian, and, therefore, more able to make your life count for God. 2. You will help the whole church to more fully reflect the praise and presence of Christ.[110] 3. You will glorify God in your serving Him and others.[111]

The real power of prayer in history is not a fusillade of praying units of whom Christ is the chief, but it is the corporate action of a Savior-Intercessor and His community, a volume of energy of prayer organized in the Holy Spirit and in the Church the Spirit creates.[112]

The workers are laborers in the local churches. In most churches, less than twenty percent of the members do one hundred percent of the work in both the nurture and mission modes. They are burning out from overload while the remaining eighty percent are rusting out as mere spectators. Usually about ninety percent of all ministry is devoted to nurture while less than ten percent is directed to mission.

---

[109] James 1:5

[110] See 1 Peter 4:10

[111] See C. Peter Wagner, *Your Spiritual Gifts Can Help Your Church Grow, How to Find Your Gifts and Use Them to Bless Others*, Regal Books, Ventura, CA, 1979, pp. 41-43.

[112] P. T. Forsyth, *The Soul of Prayer,* Eerdmans Publishing, Grand Rapids, MI, 1916, p. 55. This book can be down loaded from the internet at http://www.ccel.org/f/forsyth/soul_of_prayer/soul_of_prayer.htm

Jesus observed that, "*The harvest is plentiful but the workers are few*." Then He commanded: "*Ask the Lord of the harvest, therefore, to send out workers into his harvest field*."[113] Almost two thousand years after this promise was first given, the Christian Church has become the largest institution in the history of the world, and this growth is a concrete answer to this prayer for laborers. Where workers are needed in the harvest field, the Lord Jesus still promises to provide them. In response to prayer, God empowers and protects workers. And He will send more workers as we properly support with prayer the workers He has already sent to our church. Your intercession is as necessary as food is for your health. Without your prayers the workers in your church are like soldiers in combat without ammunition.

Almost two thousand years after this promise was first given, the Christian Church has become the largest institution in the history of the world, and this growth is a concrete answer to this prayer for laborers.

The Early Church, like a healthy body inhaling and exhaling, had a holy rhythm of nurture and mission. It gathered on the Lord's Day to be strengthened through nurture —worship, teaching, equipping, and fellowship-- ministry to the body. And then it scattered throughout the week for mission—work, mercy, service, witness, and evangelism -- ministry in and to the world. Worship means "worth-ship". Worship gives worth to work, and work provides opportunity to express worship. Through work, mercy, and service, Christians bare witness. This witness

[113] Matthew 9:37-38; also Luke 10:2

provides Christian presence, which in turn provides authenticity to gospel proclamation. Believers should daily proclaim the gospel to themselves; those who do will be more effective in proclaiming it to unbelievers.

The distinction here between witness and evangelism is important. Witness is what we are, evangelize is what we do. Witness by a life of work, mercy, and service is essential; it provides Christian presence. But Christian presence must be complemented by gospel proclamation. The U. S. Marine Corps requires every marine to qualify with a rifle. Whatever other job a marine might have, he cannot be a marine if he cannot effectively use this basic weapon. During the battle of the Chosen Reservoir I learned first hand the importance of this requirement. In Hagaru Ri the Marines were greatly outnumbered. We were being over run everywhere. Wounded men in the aid station received additional wounds and some were killed while waiting to be treated. One Marine, whose normal task was processing the bodies of those who had been killed in action, saw the enemy build up on the hilltop overlooking our emplacement. He found a truck that was loaded with ammunition and had a ring-mounted 50-caliber machine gun. He climbed on the truck and for more than five hours he fired on the enemy hoard streaming down the mountainside. At dawn, hundreds of enemy dead littered the landscape and the snow was crimson with their blood. I am alive today because this Marine knew how to fire this weapon and did his duty. God gives different natural talents and spiritual gifts to His people. However every believer should be able to proclaim the gospel.[114]

---

[114] See *Impact Your World*, "What Is the Gospel?" pp. 32-36.

Much has been written on the ministries of mercy,[115] service, and witness[116] but there is much ignorance on the ministry of what is wrongly called "secular work." I say, "wrongly called" because in the eyes of God all is sacred and nothing is secular.

Work Is Ministry

God is a worker; that's how He first appears in Scripture. In the creation account,[117] He wears no end of occupational hats: strategic planning designer, engineer, real estate developer, project manager, artist, and many more. Using these skills, He created something that was "very good."[118] Furthermore, God continues to work,[119] maintaining the creation and providing for His creatures. He also carries out the work of salvation.

God created human beings *"in His image."*[120] As His image bearers, He has placed us in authority over His creation as managers. As we use the abilities He has given us, we are His coworkers carrying out His work. We must see that God delegates His work to everybody, not just the clergy. Among the main characters of Scripture are ranchers, farmers, fishermen, ironworkers, carpenters, tentmakers, textile manufacturers, public officials,

---

[115] Timothy J. Keller, *Ministries of Mercy, The Call of the Jericho Road*, Puritan & Reformed Publishers–Phillipsburg, NJ, 1997. In addition to being an excellent work on the subject, this book contains a very helpful annotated bibliography.

[116] See bibliography in *Impact Your World,* Serve International, Atlanta, GA, 2000, pp. 177-178.

[117] See Genesis 1-2

[118] Genesis 1:37

[119] See John 5:17

[120] Genesis 1:26-27

construction supervisors and workers, military personnel, financers, physicians, judges, tax collectors, musicians, sculptors, dancers, poets, and writers. Nowhere does God view these people or their work as "second class" or "secular." Rather, their work accomplishes God's work in the world. God spent six days working on the creation[121], so we merely follow God's example when we work six days out of the week.

A biblical view of work places a high value on rest. God never intended us to work seven days a week. He calls us to join Him in a day of worship and rest, which reinforces the reality that we are His people and better helps us continue Christ's mission on this earth. This is not the place for a detailed discussion of Sabbath observance, but one comment needs to be made. The North American church is losing about 2,000 pastors each month. One reason for this loss is pastoral burnout and one of the most significant factors causing this burnout is the lack of pastors actually having one day in seven for their own personal worship and rest.

When we do our work to honor God, we will have a sense of dignity and fulfilment. As creatures made in the image of God who is a worker, we have God-given abilities to carry out important tasks that He wants done. All of this says that what we do for work and how we do it should bring glory to God. Paul urges, "*If then you were raised with Christ, seek those things which are above, where Christ is, sitting at the right hand of God. Set your mind on things above, not on things on the earth.*"[122] Working with this eternal perspective will make whatever we do spiritual

---

[121] See Genesis 1:31-2:31

[122] Colossians 3:1-2

ministry. On the other hand, without this eternal perspective everything we do, even the "religious things" will loose their spiritual value. Whatever we do should be done "*in the name of the Lord Jesus*"[123], that is, we should work in a manner that honors Him and with concern for His approval.

To the Thessalonians, Paul expressed it this way: *"Because we know that this extraordinary day is just ahead, we pray for you all the time—pray that our God will make you fit for what he's called you to be, pray that he'll fill your good ideas and acts of faith with his own energy so that it all amounts to something. If your life honors the name of Jesus, he will honor you. Grace is behind and through all of this, our God giving Himself freely, the Master, Jesus Christ, giving himself freely."* [124]

Only when the events of *this world* are seen against the reality of *that* world am I likely to think big and live big. The prayer goes on asking that God to "*fill your good ideas and acts of faith with his own energy so that it all amounts to something.*" So that you (may be glorified) in Him. Glorified Christians are those who, "*with unveiled face, beholding as in a mirror the glory of the Lord, are being transformed into the same image from glory to glory, just as by the Spirit of the Lord.*"[125]

Donald Coggan tells of an elderly black engine-man on a Great Lakes cargo boat who always kept his engine-room bright and shinny. When he was asked how he did this, he

---

[123] Colossians 3:17

[124] 2 Thessalonians 1:11-12 Eugene Peterson, *The Message: The New Testament in Contemporary Language,* Colorado Springs, CO, NavPress, 1998.

[125] 2 Corinthians 3:18

replied, "Oh! I gotta get a glory" This line comes from a spiritual that goes. . .

Oh! you gotta get a glory
In the work you do;
A Hallelujah chorus
In the heart of you.
Paint, or tell a story,
Sing or shovel coal,
But you gotta get a glory
Or the job lacks soul.

The great, whose shinning labors
Make our pulses throb,
Were men who got a glory
In their daily job.
The battle might be gory
And the odds unfair,
But the men who got a glory
Never knew despair.

Oh, Lord, give me a glory,
When all else is gone!
If you've only got a glory
You can still go on.[126]

Robert Fraley

Robert Fraley was a Christian businessman who also had "a glory." He understood and practiced this eternal perspective. From May 1990 till October 1999, I served with him on the Board of Directors of Ligonier Ministries. Robert believed that each person is called for a specific destiny as God's coworker. God endowed Robert with

[126] *The Prayers of the New Testament,* Corpus Books, Washington, DC, 1967, p. 154.

exceptional athletic ability. He was an outstanding high school athlete. In his senior year at Franklin County High School in Winchester, Tennessee, many colleges offered him a lot of incentives to go to their schools, but he chose the University of Alabama because they offered the opportunity to play under the legendary coaching of Bear Bryant. At the University of Alabama (1971-1975) he played quarterback. Physical injuries and tactical changes in the game plan limited how much he was able to play the last two seasons. When some of his friends were becoming professional athletes, Robert went to law school. Frequently his friends, who were now professional athletes, would ask Robert about their negotiations with the National Football League and Robert gave them advice. This led him to become an agent, though he hated this title because there was no professional group with established standards and many "agents" were without conscience or scruple.

He and Dixie Leigh Johnston were married in 1976. He believed it was vital to make sure that he not only loved Dixie but that he express his love in ways that clearly let her know that he loved her. For twenty-three years they had what their pastor Chuck Green called a Camelot experience.

Robert founded his company, Leader Enterprises, in 1984. By his work he consciously sought to glorify God. Eric Little was an Olympic champion whose story is told in the book and film, *Chariots of Fire*. He once said, when he ran he felt God's pleasure. Like Eric when he ran, Robert when he worked felt God's pleasure. His office was hallowed ground. This grew out of his understanding of whom God is and his own experience of God's amazing grace. He loved his clients and called them friends. He never had just a financial relationship. He wanted to serve a few selected athletes as their friend and represent them with integrity. He was always concerned about his motives. He feared he might acquiesce to the way the world operates rather than the way God wanted him to do things. He loved humility, although some close to him acknowledge that he did not always have it. His quest for truth gave him a passion for the book of Proverbs with its call to wisdom, clear thinking, and doing what is right before his God and for God's people. Robert also saw his work as his witness. He saw that *he* could most faithfully fulfill Christ's mission by serving selected athletes and the employees of his company. He planned never to retire because God didn't say work until age 60 and then play golf--God said work.

On October 25, 1999, God promoted Robert from the Church Militant to the Church Triumphant, that great throng composed of all the redeemed from every race and tongue and nation from all of history. This very private man had a very public departure from this world.

I first heard about Robert's home going from a news flash on an Atlanta radio program. The announcer spoke of a macabre scenario involving a private jet that had taken off from Orlando with the intended destination of Dallas. Six people were on board. Payne Stewart and Robert Fraley were two of the passengers on this flight. Robert and Payne were going to the Tour Championship in Houston by way of a stop in Dallas to look at the possibility of designing a golf course. At the point in their flight plan where the plane was supposed to turn west, it continued to fly north. There had been no response to attempts to communicate by radio. Now an air force fighter flying beside the jet was reporting frost inside the windows and no sign of life. This eerie situation continued until the jet ran out of fuel and plummeted to a deserted field in South Dakota.

Robert did not expect to die on October 25, 1999, but he was ready to die. Among his things in the wreckage was the book he was studying, *The Doctrine of God* by Herman Bavinck.[127] The night before the flight, Robert's last words to Dixie were "Who couldn't believe in the sovereignty of God?" If you had walked into Robert's office on that day you would have seen on his desk a copy of *God's Little Instruction Book* that was open to the page on which was written, "Leadership is a potent combination of strategy and character, but if you must be without one be without the strategy." If you had walked into the room in his home he used to workout, you would have seen on its wall a quote from Saint Augustine: "We must care for our bodies as though they were going to live forever, but we must care for our souls as if we were going to die tomorrow."

Tributes were given at Robert's funeral by Orel Hershiser, Ravi Zacharias, Paul Azinger, Tracey Stewart (Payne Stewart's wife), and Dixie Fraley; people with whom Robert lived, worked and played. These tributes reflect how well he lived with an eternal perspective.

Orel Hershiser is well known to baseball fans. He received the Cy Young Award in 1988, pitched the New York Yankees to victory in the World Series and twice has been *Sports Illustrated* sportsman of the year." Orel said, "When people ask me who is your agent? I reply, "I don't have an

---

[127] Herman Bavinck, *The Doctrine of God,* Baker Book House, Grand Rapids, MI, 1951. Bavinck was an eminent Dutch theologian and political figure at the close of the nineteenth century. This is the second volume of Bavinck's *Reformed Dogmatics.* It is a model of exhaustive and balanced Biblical exegesis, careful historical presentation, and painstaking effort to do justice to both sides of a question.

agent. I have a friend who is a believer and an attorney, and he lives in Orlando, Florida. His name is Robert Fraley. We have a deal, either I'll speak at his funeral or he'll speak at mine.

Measure life by its donation not its duration.

"Early in our relationship Robert eased a lot of my fears about playing the multiple roles of athlete, believer, husband, dreamer, investor and father. I realized very quickly I could set very high goals and risk failure, for Robert was there to guide me and to catch me if I fell. His wisdom taught me so much about the Lord, the power of being quiet and listening, honoring your word, and loving Jamie, my wife. As my play on the field excelled and our opportunity to reap financial reward increased, I will always remember what Robert said, 'You will have a successful career if at the end, you have your faith, you're still married to Jamie, your kids know you, and your reputation is in tact'."

> **"From God's perspective, death is never untimely, and it is never final; according to God, death is not a period at the end our life, rather it is a comma." Rev. Chuck Green, at Robert Fraley's funeral.**

Ravi Zacharias, international Christian leader and apologist, looking over those who were present at the funeral observed that there were many strong, muscular people, but there were also many who were not muscular and strong. Said Ravi, "This was a tribute to Robert's wide range of friendships. Robert was one who sought people out and invested his life in them. His departure from this world was a metaphor of his life. He was soaring at the height of his life then suddenly he stopped like an engine stopping in the middle of the sky."

Reflecting on what he would most miss about Robert, Ravi quoted a hymn by Thomas O. Chisholm:

> "O to be like Thee, blessed Redeemer,
> This is my constant longing and prayer.
> Gladly I'll forfeit all of earth's treasures,
> Jesus, Thy perfect likeness to bear.
> O to be like Thee, O to be like Thee,
> Blessed Redeemer, pure as Thou art,
> Come in Thy meekness, Come in Thy fullness,
> Stamp Thine own image deep on my heart.[128]

"The thing I will miss most about Robert is the stamp of Christ in him. He was a man of integrity whose friends were his heroes. How wonderful to see the heart of Christ in the heart of a man who loves and respects his friends and held them in the highest esteem.

"Time does not heal but it reveals how God heals." Dr. Ravi Zacharias at Robert Fraley's funeral.

"Dixie was the treasure of Robert's heart. How Christlike that is. Scripture tells us, 'Husbands, love your wives, just as Christ also loved the church and gave Himself for her' (Ephesians 5:25). Robert never took any invitation unless he had the option of taking Dixie. The greater hurt now in your heart is because of the greater love you enjoyed."

---

128 Thomas O. Chisholm, *O to Be Like Thee! Blessed Redeemer,* 1897.

Another who eulogized Robert was Paul Azinger. "Zinger" was PGA Player of Year (1987); eleven career wins, including '93 PGA Championship; he missed most of '94 season overcoming lymphoma in his right shoulder blade; won his first tournament since his hiatus at the Sony Open in Honolulu in January 2000. At Payne Stewart's funeral, Zinger said of Robert, "We had a professional relationship but he was first and foremost my friend, a father figure. In 1993 when I was diagnosed with cancer, Robert was the first person I called. I knew that whatever I needed, Robert would be there. Robert wrote the press release to inform the world that I had cancer. Many times during that year, Robert and Dixie proved their love for me.

"We are not in the land of the living going to the land of the dying; we are in the land of the dying going to the land of the living." Neb Hayden at Robert Fraley's funeral.

"Robert loved God and was obedient to Him, this was his highest priority. He was a man of great wisdom. When I called Robert with a question or a problem, and I had many, I had absolute confidence that his counsel would be right. He was a brilliant problem solver. He never panicked; he was always in control and always kept perspective. When I was going through chemotherapy in 1994, a lot of people called me. I tried to stay up and be a source of hope to others. One day Robert called and he said that I sounded down. I told him that I was down and that I felt bad about it. Robert responded, 'You know Paul, you don't have to be alright all the time.' This lifted a great burden from my shoulders. Robert was the best in his business. His professional direction for my life was almost flawless. He was also a servant."

Next to pay tribute was Tracey Stewart, "I thank God for Robert Fraley, our friend and our children's godfather. His wisdom and friendship was our lifeline. Robert and Payne loved being together on earth, and I'm grateful they are together now in heaven. We loved Robert and we will miss him deeply."

"Adulthood begins when a person starts to think about how he wants to be remembered." Jim Henry, Senior Pastor, First Baptist Church, Orlando at Payne Stewart's funeral.

After all others had spoken, Dixie Fraley standing between her two brothers said, "When we start a day we really have no idea how it will end. Robert and I did number our days; we just didn't know the count was so low. Robert truly loved the Lord. That did not mean he was perfect and made no mistakes. He could ruffle feathers. But he knew who the Lord was and tried to consistently see that what he believed was fleshed out in his daily behavior. He knew Truth and continually sought it. He believed that his job was to do the right thing, by the word of God and for the glory of the Lord. I live with the memories of twenty-three years of Robert's devoted love for me."

"I said to the man at the gate of the year, give me a light that I may walk safely into the unknown. And he said to me, 'Go out into the darkness and put your hand into the hand of God, it shall be to you better than the light and safer than the known'." King George VI in 1939 facing the storm clouds that became WWII. Dr. Ravi Zacharias at Robert Fraley's funeral.

Those who go into the darkness and put their hand into the hand of God will see their work as worship and witness and one day they will hear God brag on them. He will say, "*Well done, good and faithful servant; you have been faithful over a few things, I will make you ruler over many things. Enter into the joy of your lord.*" (Matthew 25:23 see also Luke 19:17).

To increase the probability of receiving this commendation from the Lord, let me suggest the following exercise. Picture yourself attending a funeral. As you walk inside the chapel, you see the flowers and hear the soft music. You see the faces of friends and family.

You walk down to the front of the room and look inside the casket where you come face to face with yourself. This is your funeral three years from today. The sanctuary is filled with people who have come to honor you, to express feelings of love and appreciation for you.

You take a seat and the service begins. You look at the printed program in your hand and see that there are to be four speakers. The first speaker is a member of your family, the second is your best friend, the third is a coworker, and the fourth is a member of the church to which you have belonged for years.

What would you like each of these speakers to say about you? What character would you like them to have seen in you? What contributions, what achievements would you want them to remember? What difference in their lives would you like to have made? Write all this in your journal, refer to it often and ask God to shape your life so that these will in fact be the things said at your funeral.[129]

[129] For a more complete explanation of this exercise, see Stephen Covey, *The 7 Habits of Highly Effective People,* Simon & Shuster, New York, 1989. See pages 95-144, "Begin with the End in Mind."

What is Vigor?

Vigor! Vitality! Strength! Without these qualities a military army engaged in war cannot be victorious. Without spiritual vigor there will be no victory in spiritual warfare. By spiritual vigor we do not mean money, political power or physical force. The term *vigor* used here refers to *the strength of the Lord and the power of His might.*[130] Only God can supply this supernatural strength to individuals and churches so that they are able to be God's people and to faithfully continue Christ's mission on earth.

In the army of saints, the strength of every individual saint, the strength of every local church outpost of saints, and the strength of a whole army of saints flow from the Lord of Hosts. One of God's names is "*the Strength of Israel.*"[131] God can overcome His enemies without our hands, but we cannot so much as defend ourselves without His arm. Jesus said, "*Without Me you can do nothing.*"[132] No holy action can be performed without the special assistance of God. "*It is God who works in you both to will and to do for His good pleasure.*"[133]

God was the strength of David's heart when, as a ruddy lad, he slew mighty Goliath, the Philistine champion, and led

---

130 Ephesians 6:10

131 1 Samuel 15:29

132 John 15:5

133 Philippians 2:13

Israel's army to victory.[134] For David, Jehovah was, "*The Lord strong and mighty, the Lord mighty in battle.*"[135] David tells us he received strength when he prayed. I "*cried out, You answered me, and made me bold with strength in my soul.*"[136] William Gurnall comments, "David did not pray himself strong, but God strengthened him in response to his prayer. God is the strength of all the saints in their war against sin and Satan."[137] David's victory revitalized the fainthearted Jewish army. They rallied and routed the Philistines.

Paul knew God's supernatural strength from personal experience. Listen to his testimony: "*And lest I should be exalted above measure by the abundance of the revelations, a thorn in the flesh was given to me, a messenger of Satan to buffet me, lest I be exalted above measure. Concerning this thing I pleaded with the Lord three times that it might depart from me. But he said to me, 'My grace is sufficient for you, for my power is made perfect in weakness.' Therefore I will boast all the more gladly about my weaknesses, so that Christ's power may rest on me. That is why, for Christ's sake, I delight in weaknesses, in insults, in hardships, in persecutions, in difficulties. For when I am weak, then I am strong.*"[138] Paul persistently prayed for the removal of Satan's messenger and finally God enabled him to glory in the presence of this thorn in the flesh; which, God explained, was sent to keep Paul humble. Having

---

[134] See 1 Samuel 17:45-47

[135] Psalm 24:8

[136] Psalm 138:3

[137] William Gurnall, *The Christian in Full Armor,* Banner of Truth, Edinburgh, Glasgow: Blackie and Son, 1864; reprint London: The Banner of Truth Trust, 1964, p. 20.

[138] 2 Corinthians 12:7-10

proven God's strength in the crucible of spiritual combat, Paul reminds us that we are not "*sufficient of ourselves to think of anything as being from ourselves, but our sufficiency is from God.*"[139]

For the Ephesian church he prayed: "I *bow my knees to the Father of our Lord Jesus Christ, from whom the whole family in heaven and earth is named, that He would grant you, according to the riches of His glory, to be strengthened with might through His Spirit in the inner man, that Christ may dwell in your hearts through faith; that you, being rooted and grounded in love, may be able to comprehend with all the saints what is the width and length and depth and height-- to know the love of Christ which passes knowledge; that you may be filled with all the fullness of God. Now to Him who is able to do exceedingly abundantly above all that we ask or think, according to the power that works in us, to Him be glory in the church by Christ Jesus to all generations, forever and ever. Amen."*[140] It is after he thus prayed that Paul commanded the Ephesian church, *"be strong in the Lord and in the power of His might.*"[141] These words encourage Christians to make use of God's almighty power as freely as if it were our own, whenever assaulted by Satan in any way.[142]

What is needed for individual and particular church vigor is the strength of the Lord. There are many factors that contribute to receiving and using this strength, but whatever else we might do to invigorate our church, we must pray with kingdom focus for its leaders and

---

139 2 Corinthians 3:5

140 Ephesians 3:14-21

141 Ephesians 6:10

142 See also Revelation 3:1-3; Isaiah 40:28-30; Deuteronomy 33:25 Nehemiah 8:10.

workers—to be the people of God and to faithfully continue Christ's mission on earth.[143] Only then can our church be vigorous enough to be all God desires her to be. Continual vigilance is essential to avoid the loss of vigor.

---

[143] The *Embers to a Flame Conferences* provide some of the best instruction available to help leaders of congregations on a statistical plateau or in decline to experience revitalization. Contact them at: embers@briarwood.org or visit the website at: www.emberstoaflame.org.

How Does a Church Lose Vigor?

Puritan pastoral theory identified four different sources for the pathology of the church that cause it to loose spiritual vigor: physical, psychological, human depravity, and demonic activity. Physical factors include things such as illness, fatigue, malnutrition or what might be called today glandular or chemical imbalance. Aging is also a physical factor. Because of its importance in today's church, we will look at this subject more fully below. Psychological factors include such issues as temperament.

Loveless comments, "The various components of spiritual pathology are often so mixed in any given crisis experience that we would be hard put to separate them, and we might be tempted simply to remain agnostic about the satanic dimension of this problem and deal with the others. But to do so would be against the example of the counsel of the apostolic church. In attempting to shield the incestuous church member at Corinth from excessive discipline after his repentance, Paul assures the Corinthians that he stands with them in forgiving him, '*lest Satan should take advantage of us; for we are not ignorant of his devices.*'[144] The designs in view here were probably oppression and accusation of this believer, the division of the church over this issue and the alienation of Paul's authority."[145]

---

[144] 2 Corinthians 2:11

[145] Richard F. Loveless, *Dynamics of Spiritual Life,* p. 140.

Fallen Human Nature

Now, let us consider human depravity as seen in the sin of fallen human nature. In the midst of Job's dialog with his friends, he states a powerful truth, "*He who has clean hands shall grow stronger and stronger.*"[146] Implicit in this statement is the opposite truth; he who has soiled hands shall become weaker and weaker. Job is not here speaking of hands covered with dirt; rather he refers to a person soiled by sin. The Westminster divines ask, "*What is sin?*" And they answer, "Sin is any lack of conformity unto, or transgression of, any law of God, given as a rule to the reasonable creature."[147]

Many insights into the nature of sin can be gained by simply considering the words used to describe it. Five Hebrew words are used in the Old Testament to describe sin: *hamas* means "a missing," *pesh* means "rebellion or transgression," *ruan* means "perversion," *rey* means "evil in disposition," and *resh* means "impiety." There are seven words in the Greek New Testament that deal with the subject of sin. *Hamartia* means, "missing the mark." It is the picture of an arrow being fired toward a target and falling short, not hitting the target. *Parabasis* means, "transgression." This presents the picture of the law as a line drawn by God. God commands man not to step over the line but man defiantly crosses, transgresses, and steps over the line. *Adika* means "contempt and violation of the law." This is the word from which we get the idea of antinomianism, that which is against the law. *Pornearia* means "depravity." We derive the English word

---

[146] Job 17:9

[147] Westminster Larger Catechism, Q. 24.

"pornography" from this Greek word. *Epithimeia* means "lust or desire for what is forbidden."

The English language provides a wide range of words for the concept of sin: transgression, trespass, violation, impiety, profaneness, blasphemy, desecration, irreverence, ungodliness, wrong, wickedness, immorality, iniquity, evil, error, guilt, offense, crime, fault, omission, shortcoming and mistake. These are only a few of the words.

The formers of the Westminster standards defined sin as "any want of conformity unto …the law of God." This indicates sins of omission—not doing what Scripture says we should do. For example, any person who is not using his or her spiritual gifts is sinning.[148] In some cases this may be doing ministry for which one is not gifted. Also prayerlessness is sin.[149] Prayer is a means of grace. Therefore, when it is neglected it results in loss of power. One of the devil's chief strategies is to use the good as the enemy of the best.

Westminster continues its definition of sin as "transgression of the law of God" meaning sins of commission, doing what God's law forbids. Questions 150 and 151 of The Larger Catechism deal with the various impact of sin in the sight of God.

> **Q. 150. Are all transgressions of the law of God equally heinous (i.e., hateful) in themselves and in the sight of God?**
> **A.** All transgressions of the law of God are not equally heinous; but some sins in themselves,

148 See Luke 19:11-27

149 See 1 Samuel 12:23

and by reason of several aggravations (*i.e.*, many irritations), are more heinous in the sight of God than others.

Q. 151. What are those aggravations that make some sins more heinous than others?
A. Sins receive their aggravations,
1. From the persons offending; if they be of riper age, greater experience or grace, eminent for profession, gifts, place, office, guides to others, and whose example is likely to be followed by others.
2. From the parties offended: if immediately against God, his attributes, and worship; against Christ, and his grace; the Holy Spirit, his witness, and workings; against superiors, men of eminency, and such as we stand especially related and engaged unto; against any of the saints, particularly weak brethren, the souls of them, or any other, and the common good of all or many.
3. From the nature and quality of the offence: if it be against the express letter of the law, break many commandments, contain in it many sins: if not only conceived in the heart, but breaks forth in words and actions, scandalize others, and admit of no reparation: if against means, mercies, judgments, light of nature, conviction of conscience, public or private admonition, censures of the church, civil punishments; and our prayers, purposes, promises, vows, covenants, and engagements to God or men: if done deliberately, willfully, presumptuously, impudently, boastingly, maliciously, frequently, obstinately, with

> delight, continuance, or relapsing after repentance.
> **From circumstances of time and place**: if on the Lord's day, or other times of divine worship; or immediately before or after these, or other helps to prevent or remedy such miscarriages: if in public, or in the presence of others, who are thereby likely to be provoked or defiled.

Periodic prayerful meditation on these two questions and their answers will help us understand how serious sin truly is.

I once heard a standup comedian describe his first parachute jump: "I jumped from the airplane at 2,000 feet and pulled the ripcord but nothing happened. As I hurtled toward the ground all my past sins flashed before my eyes, but finally at about 800 feet the chute opened, and I floated safely to the ground. Do you know what I did then? I got in the airplane and jumped ten more times because I enjoyed my sins so much." The comedian continued, "God and I have an arrangement. He likes to forgive sin, and I like to sin."

The devil tries to make us laugh at our sin but God says, *"Woe to those who call evil good, and good evil; Who put darkness for light, and light for darkness; Who put bitter for sweet, and sweet for bitter!"*[150] God further says, *"He who covers his sins will not prosper, but whoever confesses and forsakes them will have mercy."*[151]

---

[150] Isaiah 5:20

[151] Proverbs 28:13

Richard Lovelace in 1974, to describe the discrepancy between what Christians say they believe and how they behave, coined the phrase, "sanctification gap". In 2001, George Barna tells us, "Expect the gap between our verbalized values (what we say) and our practiced values (what we do) to grow wider and wider."[152] It is at the points where the "gap" is the greatest in personal life or congregational life that God allows Satan to sift His saints.[153]

The Christian who is substantially walking in light through loving obedience to God's Word is practically invulnerable to the assaults of darkness as Jesus intimates in the parable of the empty house.[154] This is beautifully expressed in John Bunyan's allegory, *Pilgrim's Progress.* He pictures the powers of darkness as lions chained on a short tether on either side of the road to the Celestial City. These lions can maul travelers who wander from the middle of the path, but the lion cannot touch those who walk precisely in the center.[155]

---

152 Barna and Hatch , *Boiling Point, It Only Takes One Degree,* p. 24.

153 For a further explanation of the satanic sifting concept see below, pp. 93-96.

154 See Matthew 12:43-45

155 "So I saw in my dream, that he made haste and went forward, that if possible he might get lodging there. Now before he had gone far, he entered into a very narrow passage, which was about a furlong off of the Porter's Lodge, and looking very narrowly before him as he went, he espied two lions in the way. Now, thought he, I see the dangers that Mistrust and Timorous were driven back by, (The lions were chained, but he saw not the chains.). Then he was afraid and thought also himself to go back after him, for he thought nothing but death was before him: but the porter at the lodge, whose name is Watchful, perceiving that Christian made a halt, as if he would go back, cried unto him saying, Is thy strength so small? Fear not the lions, for they are chained; and are placed there for trial of faith where it is; and for discovery of those who have none: keep in the midst of the path, and no hurt will come unto thee.

Believers should not be arrogant or show an offhanded cavalier disregard for sin. God will not tolerate His children willfully, premeditatedly, practicing sin. In fact, He may discipline it by taking the physical life of the offender. The writer of Proverbs warned: "*Harsh discipline is for him who forsakes the way, and he who hates correction will die.*"[156] The Apostle Paul admonished the Corinthian Church that their abuse of the Lord's Supper caused many to be, "*weak and sick among you, and many sleep.*"[157] This physical situation reflected the spiritual reality. Paul also urged the Corinthian Church to discipline blatant sexual immorality among them by delivering the offender "*to Satan for the destruction of the flesh, that his spirit may be saved in the day of the Lord Jesus*".[158] John, the beloved disciple tells us, "*If anyone sees his brother sinning a sin which does not lead to death, he will ask, and He will give him life for those who commit sin not leading to death. There is sin leading to death. I do not say that he should pray about that. All unrighteousness is sin, and there is sin not leading to death.*"[159] As we said above, God will not tolerate His children willfully, premeditatedly, practicing sin. In fact, He may discipline the practice of sin by taking the physical life of the offender.

"The I saw that he went on, trembling for fear of the lions; but taking good heed to the directions of the porter; he heard them roar, but they did him no harm." *The Pilgrim's Progress, from this World to that which is to Come,* by John Bunyon, Edited by James Blanton Wharley, 2nd Edition, Revised by Roger Sharrock, London, Oxford University Press, 1960, p. 45-46.

156 Proverbs 15:10

157 1 Corinthians 11:30

158 1 Corinthians 5:1-5

159 1 John 5:16-17

God will not tolerate His children willfully, premeditatedly, practicing sin. In fact, He may discipline the practice of sin by taking the physical life of the offender.

Because God loves His children, He chastens them when they sin. Scripture says,

> *"My son, do not despise the chastening of the Lord, nor be discouraged when you are rebuked by Him; for whom the Lord loves He chastens, and scourges every son whom He receives.*
> *"If you endure chastening, God deals with you as with sons; for what son is there whom a father does not chasten? But if you are without chastening, of which all have become partakers, then you are illegitimate and not sons. Furthermore, we have had human fathers who corrected us, and we paid them respect. Shall we not much more readily be in subjection to the Father of spirits and live? For they indeed for a few days chastened us as seemed best to them, but He for our profit, that we may be partakers of His holiness. Now no chastening seems to be joyful for the present, but painful; nevertheless, afterward it yields the peaceable fruit of righteousness to those who have been trained by it."*[160]

God not only chastens individuals but whole congregations. The church in Thyatira was guilty of practicing sexual immorality and idolatry. Christ warned them, *"I will kill*

---

160 Hebrews 12:6-11

her children with death".[161] While the church in Sardis had a reputation of being alive and active, in reality it was close to death. Jesus commands, *"Be watchful, and strengthen the things which remain, that are ready to die, for I have not found your works perfect before God. Remember therefore how you have received and heard; hold fast and repent".* [162] And to the church of the Laodiceans the glorified Christ said, *"As many as I love, I rebuke and chasten. Therefore be zealous and repent".*[163]

The Sin of Self Confidence

One sin worthy of special consideration is the sin of self-confidence. At the last supper, Peter said to Jesus, "Even if all are made to stumble, yet I will not be." Jesus said to him, "Assuredly, I say to you that today, even this night, before the rooster crows twice, you will deny Me three times." But he spoke more vehemently, "If I have to die with You, I will not deny You!" And they all said likewise."[164] Only hours later Jesus, "found them sleeping, and said to Peter, 'Simon, are you sleeping? Could you not watch one hour? Watch and pray, lest you enter into temptation. The spirit indeed is willing, but the flesh is weak.'"[165] The remedy for self-confidence is reliance on God, the Holy Spirit. Prayer is an admission of human inability and an appropriation of divine omnipotence.

---

[161] Revelation 2: 23

[162] Revelation 3:1-3

[163] Revelation 3:19

[164] Mark 14:29-31 parallel Matthew 26:33-35

[165] Mark 14:37-38 parallel Matthew 26:40-41

Racial, Social, or Economic Discrimination

As the apostles moved from the upper room and set out to continue Christ's mission to the uttermost parts of the earth, the believing communities they established constantly broke down the world's boundaries of nation, race, language, class, and culture. One major factor that drains vigor from American churches today is a pervasive presence of discrimination based on race, social status or economic level. Neighborhoods are constantly changing and many existing churches do not minister to the new comers. When this happens, the blessing of God may be withdrawn. Changing neighborhoods promise to be a growing challenge. Barna reports, "No longer does America's population expansion rely upon whites having babies. The white population, while still the majority, reflects a declining share of the nation's citizenry; formerly comprising more 80 percent of the nation's people, whites now constitute 72 percent of the population, and will decline to about 68 percent by 2010 and will be barely half of the population by 2050!"[166]

When God plants a church He always desires that it be indigenous, originating, growing and living in a specific geographic area and environment. The church on earth should be patterned after the church in heaven. *"After these things I looked, and behold, a great multitude which no one could number, of all nations, tribes, peoples, and tongues, standing before the throne and before the Lamb, clothed with white robes, with palm branches in their hands, and crying out with a loud voice, saying, 'Salvation belongs to our God who sits on the throne, and to the Lamb!'"*[167]

---

[166] Barna and Hatch, *Boiling Point, It only Takes One Degree,* p. 33.
[167] Revelation 7:9-10; See also Ephesians 2:11-22

According to Danny Sanchez, director of the Scarborough Institute for Church Growth at Southwestern Baptist Seminary, "America is the most culturally diversified nation in the world today." Ethnic growth in the past decade has been tremendous in the United States: Asian 107%, Hispanic 53%, Native American 38%, African American 16.3% increase. This takes on significance when we understand that the general population has only grown by 6% in the last decade. In spite of these trends, "Nearly 90 percent of Americans who call themselves evangelicals are white."[168] Many churches have closed their doors and many more have ceased to function as churches—being the people of God and faithfully continuing the mission of Christ—because they did not maintain a biblically congruent and healthy relationship with the changing demographics of the community around them.

When God plants a church He always desires that it be indigenous, originating, growing and living in a specific geographic area and environment.

Two extremes on the ministry path expose a congregation and each individual in it to the Satan's sifting work. On one side is *cultural insensitivity* and on the other is *cultural idolatry. Cultural insensitivity* is the result of too *little* emphasis on group distinctives. This will cause the church to unconsciously exalt the ways and customs of one or two groups over others and will determine that outreach will be ineffective. Each distinct group and culture has a God-given authenticity. The other extreme is *Cultural idolatry*, concerning which Tim Keller states: "Too much emphasis

---

[168] Michael O. Emerson and Christian Smith, *Divided by Faith*, Oxford University Press, 2000, p. 3.

on distinct 'peopleness' (cultural identity) overlooks the fact that all natural group identities have an idolatrous aspect—they are substitutes for Christ and his Body. Every people group 'has a demonic side as well as God-given authenticity', and to exalt it too highly is to 'stress the pluriformity of the church more than its catholicity (its universality)' . . . If breaking down barriers between separate people in the world is an essential part of the gospel, *not merely a result of it*, doesn't an overemphasis on 'people groups' inhibit the expression of gospel 'oneness'?"

When we approach new people groups outside the church, the Bible tells us to be very sensitive to their differences and to consider how outsiders will perceive our behavior and hear our message.[169]

It is a universal fact that people are naturally most "comfortable" with people who are like themselves. This desire for comfort can move people to under-adapt to new people groups. People usually refuse to adapt to new people groups because they are clinging to the superiority of their race and culture out of spiritual insecurity. Richard Loveless correctly comments:

> "Those who are not secure in Christ cast about for spiritual life preservers with which to support their confidence, and in their frantic search they may not only cling to the shreds of ability and righteousness they find in themselves, but they fix upon their race, their membership in a party, their familiar social and ecclesiastical patterns, and their

[169] See I Thessalonians 4:11-12; I Corinthians 14:23; Colossians 4:5

> culture as means of self-recommendation. The culture is put on as though it were armor against self-doubt, but it becomes a mental straightjacket which cleaves to the flesh and can never be removed except through comprehensive faith in the saving work of Christ. Once faith is exercised, a Christian is free to be acculturated, to wear his culture like a comfortable suit of clothes. He can shift to another cultural clothing temporarily if he wishes to do so, as Paul suggests in 1 Corinthians 9:19-23, and he is released to admire and appreciate the differing expressions of Christ shinning out through other cultures."[170]

All Christians are really foreigners and aliens on earth![171] We must pray for and practice a willingness to be vulnerable and teachable. As we pray and intentionally interact with people of other "*ethne*" around us, God will change us into the image of His Son, who during His earthly ministry, went out of His way to minister cross culturally.[172]

Let us turn now to the exploration of the challenge of aging.

Aging Members and Congregations

Aging of individual members and congregations is another factor draining vigor from the church. George Barna

---

[170] Loveless, *Dynamics of Spiritual Life,* pp. 198-199.

[171] See Acts 7:6,29; Ephesians 2:19; I Peter 2:11; Romans 12:1-2

[172] See John 4

informs us, “America’s population is getting older. Just a few decades ago our median age was near 30; presently it is in the mid-30s and will continue to climb during this decade. The major reason is the growth in the numbers of people 65 and older.”[173] Barna further observes, “Congregations will become older, on average, as the decade progresses. This will be attributable to a large percentage of young adults—Busters and Mosaics—avoiding physical churches for alternate church models (e.g., house churches, cyberchurches) and many engaging in spiritual anarchy (i.e., doing whatever works at the moment, without any sense of parameters or obligation to belong to an organized group of like-minded people).”[174]

Individual and organizational aging is inevitable and properly dealing with the changes produced by aging can increase church vigor. However, improperly dealing with these challenges will cause the church to fall short of God’s desires for it and falling short is sin.[175] Sin always robs individuals and their local churches of vigorous, effective ministry. Thus the American church is facing a significant challenge in the next ten years with our aging population. As members grow older they slow down physically. Modern Americans seeking to avoid loss of vigor, refuse to be bound by traditional age limitations. This trend is called “Down-Aging.” The same baby boom bunches that once said, don’t trust anyone over thirty, now says, with equal militancy, “Life begins at forty.” Americans spend $2 billion a year on products to ward off aging; forty now is what used to be thirty, fifty now is what used to be forty, sixty-five now is the beginning of the second half of life.

---

173 Barna and Hatch, *Boiling Point, It only Takes One Degree,* p. 34-35.

174 Ibid., 227.

175 See Romans 3:23

Down aging is driven by age arrogance; the sheer numbers of the group and a deep-felt need to laugh. We are turning, as often as we can, into big goofy kids, and the release it affords. Down aging is the bridge by which adults of all ages try to connect the carefree childhoods we remember (or at least the carefree baby-boom childhoods the media says we're supposed to remember) to the not-so-always-fun adulthood we find ourselves in now. We're spending more money now on recreation than clothing. Having enough money for retirement is the number-one financial worry for people aged 35-49. This generation will grow old with a stylish vengeance, putting in more energy against growing old, and the way growing old makes us feel, than any generation in history.

Our society places a decisive accent on youth and evokes a corresponding fear of old age. The increase in the number of elderly has paralleled a decrease in their role and status. Youth is placed on a pedestal as to amount to "idolization." Americans are obsessed with escaping the fate of physical deterioration from growing old—cosmetic surgery, hair-dyeing, new wardrobes. People in their forties are still referred to as "young men." People in their sixties are "mature," getting along in years," "senior citizens," or "golden agers," but they are not aged or old.[176] Longfellow provides encouragement for graying baby bombers.

---

176 See "Down Aging," Faith Popcorn, *The Popcorn Report,* Doubleday, New York, 1991, p. 56-61.

"It is too late!" Ah nothing is too late—
Cato learned Greek at eighty; Sophocles
Wrote his grand "Oedipus", and Simonides
Bore off the prize of verse from his compeers
When each had numbered more than fourscore years;
And Theophrastus, at fourscore and ten,
Had begun his "Characters of Men".
Chaucer, at Woodstock, with his nightingales,
At sixty wrote the "Canterbury Tales".
Goethe, at Weimar, toiling to the last,
Completed "Faust" when eighty years were past.
What then? Shall we sit idly down and say,
"The night has come; it is no longer day"?
For age is opportunity no less
Than youth itself, though in another dress.
And as the evening twilight fades away,
The sky is filled with stars, invisible by day.[177]

The Bible, in contrast with our culture, emphasizes reaching our prime spiritually, psychologically, and mentally as we age. Older people in the Bible were not made to feel that they ought to apologize for being alive. Aging was a cause for celebration; indeed, to be older was better. If our theology is incorrect, our sociology can hardly be right. Aging will always bring about a decline of physical vigor. We are to honor those who are older than we are. We are to provide care for the elderly. And we are to seek out our elders for the wisdom of their years.

Rabbinic literature also stress the importance of old people as a source of wisdom: "He who learns from the young is like one who eats unripe grapes and drinks wine from the winepress. But he who learns from the old is like one who

---

[177] Henry Wadsworth Longfellow

eats ripe grapes and drinks old wine." Every age group from five years of age to one hundred— has its special function within the community: At five years old (one is ready) for the study of Scripture, at ten for the Mishnah, at thirteen for (the fulfilling of) the commandments, at fifteen for the Talmud, at eighteen for marriage, at twenty for the pursuit of a livelihood, at thirty (man reaches) full strength, at forty full understanding, at fifty able to give counsel, at sixty for old age (that is to be an elder), at seventy for gray hair, at eighty his survival reflects special strength, at ninety for a bent body, and at 100 he is as good as dead and passed away and ceased from the world.[178]

The Bible provides us an example of one who kept both his physical and his spiritual vigor to the end of his life. Caleb was born a slave, served as a spy, and survived a forty year trek in the desert. Then at the age of 85, he led the defeat of guerrilla fighters in the mountains and provided an inheritance for his family. In his generation, he was one of only two men who escaped God's judgment. Caleb followed God's providence rather than try to force it. And he did not follow with selective obedience or by fits and starts, but he followed constantly because he was a rooted man. Forty-five years he lived in the camp of Israel—never once consorting with the murmuring rebels.

Caleb was a brave man among cowards, an assured man among skeptics. His life teaches very valuable lessons concerning growing older in grace. First, laying claim to our inheritance may involve us in new conflicts late in life but it is possible that life's greatest achievements will take place in old age. Second, consistent obedience is costly but it increases moral vigor. Third, fidelity to God's commands

---

[178] Abot 5:21 quoted in Marvin Wilson, *Our Father Abraham,* Eerdmans, Grand Rapids, 1989, p. 230.

enriches the whole of life. Fourth, complete victory demands unreserved obedience. Fifth, there is no retiring age in the service of God.

Each of these lessons has application to the church of today. The older members should encourage the younger. If history is any indicator, when revival comes it will probably be led by men under thirty years of age. Evan Roberts was only twenty-four when God used him to launch the Welch Revival. Other young men and women flocked around him and encouraged him, but many of the older established church leaders at best ignored him and at worst attacked both him and the work God was doing. Eighteen months into the revival, Evan was scheduled to speak and more than five thousand turned out for the meeting. When young Evan (then twenty-five) entered the hall a whisper went through the audience, "Evan is here!" Then the entire group stood in quiet reverence. Evan looked at the multitude, and then he said to his companion, "I have touched the glory of God!" He walked out of the hall and never again appeared in public. The elders of the church then went to him and pleaded for him to continue with the Lord's work, but he refused.

Many times I have told this story to congregations and it has led to dialog with the young men. I have asked these young men what they would like for my generation to do to help them with their spiritual responsibilities. The answer is usually the same: "Share your experience with us. Tell us the principles you have learned from these experiences. Then pray for us and encourage us to apply the principles as God guides us in our ministry."

It is alarming to me to see the large number of older people who were once very active in the church now doing nothing. What one does at seventy will certainly be different than what one did at thirty. We must work smarter rather than harder. The most significant ministry for today's older Christians may be intercession for those who are in face-to-face combat with the forces of evil.

There is another extreme that needs also to be addressed. Some older saints caught up in the "Down-Aging" craziness of our culture, try to hang on to their youth by refusing to relinquish the controls to ministry. I believe ministry should be like parenting: a good parent works to see that his children greatly surpass what ever he as a parent might have achieved in the work of the Lord. Likewise, leaders and workers in churches should live by the motto: "There is no success in ministry without successors."

As churches age, their structure usually become less flexible and tends to stifle ministry rather than facilitate it.

Structural Renewal

Studies of business organizations show that they may go through five phases of organization development. The age and size of the organization play a significant role in the evolutionary periods of gradual growth and the revolutionary periods of rapid growth of the organization. Growth rate of the industry (in this case, the church of a region or the nation) is also a factor. The five key phases are: 1. Growth through creativity that causes a crisis of leadership. 2. Growth through direction that creates a crisis of autonomy. 3. Growth through delegation causing a crisis of control. 4. Growth through delegation resulting in a crisis of red tape. 5. Growth through collaboration causing a crisis of new structures and programs that allow employees to periodically rest, reflect, and revitalize themselves.[179] Exhibit I shows this process in graphic form.

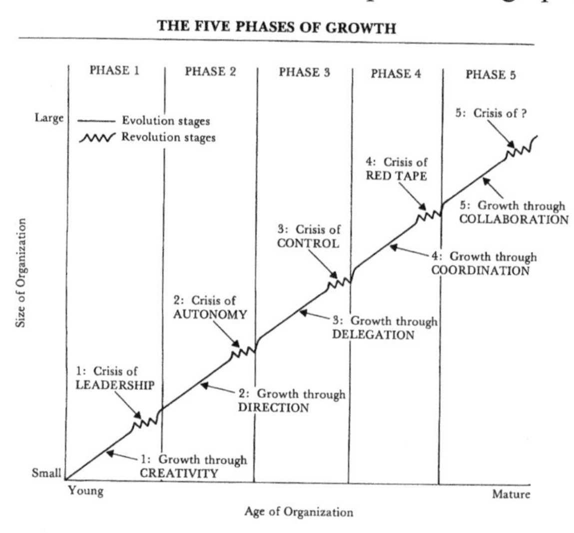

The church is more than a human organization but as a human organization, some of these factors contribute to the corporate vitality or lack of it. It is sufficient here to emphasize that leaders and workers in local churches need to understand that the structural vigor of the local church is not merely the sum total of the vigor of the individual members of the church.

Richard Loveless agrees: “It is not enough to renew individual hearts for churches to be renewed, although it is probably true that structural renewal cannot progress very far unless it is preceded by a great deal of individual awakening. Because individual Christians—and even local congregations—are not ultimate ends in themselves, but cells in the body of Christ, reconstitution of these cells is

---

179 Larry E. Greiner, "Evolution and Revolution as Organizations Grow," *Harvard Business Review,* Cambridge, MA, July-August 1972.

often necessary for spiritual health and fullness of Christ to be present in the church."[180]

In a vital church, the minister is not a dominant superstar who specializes in the spiritual concerns of the Christian community, while the laity are free to go about their own business because the pastor is taking care of the business of the kingdom. This type of ministry defies the biblical concept of the priesthood of all believers.

Loveless more than twenty-five years ago wrote:

> "The American church has degenerated into folk religion or moralism. Patterns of lay passivity and pastoral dominance must be broken. This will require a certain relinquishment of power in democratizing the congregational pattern; pastors must decrease in order that the laity may increase. Since some ministers are using their congregations as private kingdoms which contribute to their own emotional support, this will require a thorough work of the cross in renewing the pastor's own life."[181]

---

180 Loveless, *Dynamics of Spiritual Life,* p. 223.

181 Ibid., 224.

How Does a Church Regain Vigor?

Faith begins in stillness of heart, and it must constantly be returning to quiet communion with God. "But," observes Helmut Thieliche, "when it remains only on the inside, it decomposes, and becomes a musty, unventilated piety. On the other hand, when it seeks only the outside it withers and becomes sterile in a Christian busyness that is cut off from the eternal springs. Even a growing tree enlarges its invisible roots in proportion as it increases its visible form.

"We people of today, who usually have so terrible much to do, we, of all people, should realize that we can permit ourselves to be visible and public only in proportion as we sink deeper roots into the earth and through ever increasing roots absorb the strength of eternity and the peace of God."[182]

Elton Trueblood adds to this, "Only by a conscious and continuing nurture of his inner life can any man avoid the tragedy of killing the thing he loves. The man who supposes that he has not time to pray or to reflect because the social tasks are so numerous and urgent will soon find that he has become fundamentally unproductive because he has separated his life from its roots.

"It will not be surprising then, if, in his promotion of what seems to him to be a good cause, he becomes bitter in his

---

[182] Helmut Thieliche, *The Trouble with the Church: A Call for Renewal,* Grand Rapids, MI, Baker Book House, 1965, p. 75.

condemnation of others. Without the concurrent cultivation of the inner and the outer life, it is almost inevitable that a man deeply involved in social action should become self-righteous."[183]

When vigor is lost, it can be regained. Six elements in the process of regaining vigor are: Periodic self-examination, repentance, periodic extraordinary prayer, spying out the land, renewing structure, and dividing and delegating the work.

Periodic Self-Examination

The cultivation of the inner life requires periodic self-examination. The Apostle Paul urged each Corinthian Christian when he or she came to the Lord's Table to individually, "*examine himself.*"[184] In this same context, he promises, "*if we judged ourselves rightly, we should not be judged.*"[185] Begin with the Psalmist's prayer "*Search me, O God, and know my heart; try me, and know my anxieties; and see if there is any wicked way in me, and lead me in the way everlasting.*"[186]

Keep in mind God's goal for His whole Church: "*to show his wisdom in all its rich variety to all the rulers and authorities in the heavenly realms. They will see this when Jews and Gentiles are joined together in his church. This was his plan from all eternity, and it has now been carried out through Christ Jesus our Lord.*"[187] Also remember His

---

[183] Elton Trueblood, *New Man for Our Time*, Harper & Row, New York, 1970, p. 60.

[184] 1 Corinthians 11:28

[185] 1 Corinthians 11:31 NASB

[186] Psalm 139:23, 24

[187] Ephesians 3:8-11 NLT

purpose for you: "*For whom He foreknew, He also predestined to become conformed to the image of His Son, that He might be the first-born among many brethren.*"[188] God's Word is the standard by which we must examine ourselves: "*For the word of God is living and powerful, and sharper than any two-edged sword, piercing even to the division of soul and spirit, and of joints and marrow, and is a discerner of the thoughts and intents of the heart.*"[189]

Every person has a variety of roles. Roles are the operations expected as we relate to other persons in the performance of daily duties. For example, in your relationship with God you are His worshipper and servant. If you are committed to the Lord, you are the enemy of the devil. In your family relationship you are son or daughter, father or mother, brother or sister. In your work relationships you are employer or employee or fellow worker, customer, client, vender, competitor, etc. Figure 1 shows the relationship between the dimensions of a person and his or her roles.

[188] Romans 8:29

[189] Hebrews 4: 12

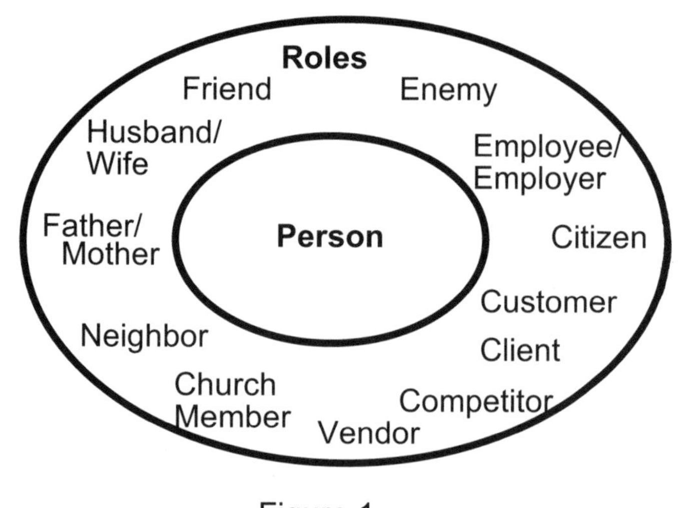

Figure 1

Repentance

Pause in your reading now and do the following exercise. Identify your roles, list the names of all who relate to you in these various roles. Then evaluate your relationships by asking: "What in this relationship pleases the Lord?" Thank God for each thing that is pleasing to the Lord.

By the way, since the church will ultimately be "*a great multitude which no one could number, of all nations, tribes, peoples, and tongues*,"[190] it makes sense that God would be very pleased if some of your relationships were with people of a race and socioeconomic group other than your own.

---

[190] Revelation 7:9-10

Next ask: "What in this relationship does not please the Lord?" After you complete your list of things not pleasing to the Lord, review it and ask God to show you *why* each specific thing is there. This will usually reveal other factors in your life with which you need to deal. Continue this process until you discover the cause of any sin in the relationship. In this way you will get to the root of your sin. Never settle for dealing superficially with the fruit of sin. Only when you attack it at the root will you find real victory.

When I went through this exercise, the Holy Spirit deeply convicted me of racism, not active racism but passive racism. I did not utter racial slurs but I listened to jokes that demeaned brothers of color and did not rebuke the one telling the joke. Actually I thought I was without prejudice until I spent more time with brothers of color and worked at seeing reality through their eyes. My racism was rooted in ignorance, and I did not know what I did not know.
When a significant number of church members take this matter of sin in their relationships seriously and then act on this sin in a biblical manner, the local church will be more likely to experience corporate renewal.

Once sin (both the roots and the fruits) is identified, repent of it. God repeatedly calls for repentance.[191] The Greek word for repentance is *metanoia.* It literally means to turn the head, to change your mind. If you turn your head, the body has to follow. If the head turns around, and the body

---

[191] Or do you despise the riches of His goodness, forbearance, and longsuffering, not knowing that the goodness of God leads you to repentance? (Romans 2:4). For godly sorrow produces repentance leading to salvation, not to be regretted; but the sorrow of the world produces death. (2 Corinthians 7:10 see also Ezekiel 18:30,32; 33:11; Acts 2:37,38; 3:19; 20:21; 26:20) 2 Corinthians 7:10

goes in the other direction, you are in trouble. Repentance is related to the idea "convert" which means to turn around. Repentance is like a U-turn on the road of life. It denotes a change of outlook, a new direction in life that involves turning toward God and away from sin. God says, *"He who covers his sins will not prosper, but whoever confesses and forsakes them will have mercy."*[192] .

The whole person (mind, affections, and will) has to be involved in repentance. With the mind, you must know that you have no hope in yourself. Your heart must be broken and contrite because of your sin. Your will must desire to trust. You must move away from reliance on yourself to trust in Christ. You must be willing to turn from anything that God says is wrong.

By repentance sinners see and understand the danger of their situation. They also become aware of their sin's filth and stench. Their sin is understood as contrary to the holy nature and righteous law of God. They see that their only hope is in God's mercy in Christ to such as are penitent. They grieve for and hate their sins so as to turn from them unto God. They purpose and endeavor to walk with God in all the ways of His commandments.

As there is no sin so small but it deserves damnation; so there is no sin so great that it can bring damnation upon those who truly repent. Christians ought *not* to content themselves with a general repentance, but it is every person's duty to endeavor to repent of his or her particular sins, particularly. One who is genuinely repentant will

---

[192] Proverbs 28:13

perform three acts that demonstrate the reality of his penitence. He or she will confess, repay and watch.[193]

1. Confess

Sincere penitence must lead to confession. To confess means to agree with God that what He calls sin is sin. God can forgive sin but He will not give the sense of forgiveness if we rationalize sin and call it something else—like mistakes. Confession must come from the heart. *"Out of the abundance of the heart the mouth speaks."*[194]

Every sin is first and foremost an offense against a holy God. David committed adultery and arranged for Uriah to be killed. Under the Spirit's inspiration David prayed to the Lord, "*Against You, You only, have I sinned, and done this evil in Your sight-- That You may be found just when You speak, and blameless when You judge*."[195] Therefore, our first responsibility is to confess our sin to God in private prayer. True repentance will always thus express itself to the Lord.

If our sin impacts another person and we know it, repentance will lead to confessing to the wronged person. Jesus commanded, "*Therefore if you bring your gift to the altar, and there remember that your brother has something against you, leave your gift there before the altar, and go your way. First be reconciled to your brother, and then come and offer your gift*."[196] Some sins are private and only the sinner and the offended person are aware of them. Other sins are public and scandalous. If our sins are public

---

[193] Also see C. Jack Miller, *Repentance & 20th Century Man,* Christian Literature Crusade, Fort Washington, PA, 1975.

[194] Matthew 12:34

[195] Psalm 51:4

[196] Matthew 5:23, 24

and have scandalized Christ and the Church, public confession is biblically necessary.[197]

Scripture indicates that local churches are responsible for the discipline of their members. In the Church to which I belong members vow to submit themselves to the discipline of the church as taught in Scripture. Our leaders make sure this is understood when individuals first unite with the congregation. Loving, firm, and consistent discipline is essential for the unity, purity, holiness, and apostolicity of each local church. Proper church discipline is not a witch-hunt. It always has as its objective the exoneration of the name of Christ, the restoration of the sinner, and the strengthening of the church.

2. <u>Repay</u>

By "repay" I mean making restitution, attempting to repair the damage our sins have caused whenever it is possible. As God was drawing me to trust Christ, I was overwhelmed by the load of guilt. I told this to a pastor and he asked me what I'd done to feel so guilty. I listed every sin I could remember. When I paused, he urged me to pray with him. With great fervor, he interceded for me--but I felt no release from my sin. I told him what we were doing was not working. He said maybe I needed to do restitution. This was a new word for me so I asked what it meant. He said restitution means you make right the things you have done wrong.

I gasped! The most gruesome of my past sins flashed through my mind. I said, "You have got to be kidding. How do I go back to Korea and give life to men I killed two years ago?"

---

[197] See I Timothy 5:20

He said, "I don't know what to tell you, but I'll pray for you." I left that man with a sense of total hopeless despair!

Looking back on this dark moment, I wish the man had explained what the Bible teaches about restitution. Moses taught,

> *If anyone sins against me (the Lord) by refusing to return a deposit on something borrowed or rented, or by refusing to return something entrusted to him, or by robbery, or by oppressing his neighbor, or by finding a lost article and lying about it, swearing that he doesn't have it - on the day he is found guilty of any such sin, he shall restore what he took, adding twenty percent fine, and give it to the one he has harmed.*[198]

> *Tell the people of Israel that when anyone, man or woman, betrays the Lord by betraying a trust, it is sin. He must confess his sin and make full repayment for what he has stolen, adding twenty percent and returning it to the person he took it from. But if the person he wronged is dead, and there is no near relative to whom the payment can be made, it must be given to the priest, along with a lamb for atonement.*[199]

A person who truly repents sincerely wishes he had never sinned and desires the damage to be as little as possible. Therefore, he will seek to minimize the damage, if it is in his power. This is what John the Baptist demanded of the Pharisees. This is what happened when the Lord confronted

[198] Leviticus 6:2-4 LB

[199] Numbers 5:5-8 LB

Zacchaeus and he donated half his goods to the poor (Jewish law required only a fifth). Christ saw in this evidence of genuine repentance.[200] These works of restitution do not save, but they demonstrate that repentance is genuine.

Making restitution can provide fruitful opportunity for witness. When Christians contact individuals they have sinned against, ask their forgiveness, and seek to repair past damage, incredible things happen. Unbelievers want to know what in the world made the believer ask his forgiveness and try to correct the wrong. This provides powerful opportunities to tell of the love of Christ.

For example, shortly after Lee and Linda were married, they learned the Bible's teaching on restitution. Both of them had been sexually involved with others before God brought them to Himself and to one another. Each of them, with the other present, contacted by phone each person with whom they had immoral relations, explained that they had become Christians and asked forgiveness for the past. The standard response received was, "You obviously have found something very powerful for your life. I wish you well." In a few situations, the person from the past asked if they could get together to talk further about how they could find this same kind of relationship. Believers like Lee and Linda receive a depth of freedom in their own spirits that is incredible. Satan has less ground to accuse them.

Sometimes the damage caused by our sin is *not* repairable. Saul of Tarsus was responsible for the death of the Stephen, the first Christian martyr.[201] God forgave him and made

---

200 See Luke 19:8,9

201 See Acts 8:1-2.

him into the most effective proclaimer of grace the world has ever seen. David committed adultery and conspired to murder; his repentance did not undo his adultery nor did it restore Uriah's life. His sense of guilt was unbearable until he repented and confessed his sin to God.[202] Then David could exclaim, "*Blessed is he whose transgressions are forgiven, whose sins are covered. Blessed is the man whose sin the LORD does not count against him and in whose spirit is no deceit.*"[203]

Be aware that the devil (the accuser of the brethren) will try to use sins we cannot repair to cripple us.[204] God forgives our sins and remembers them no more.[205] The grace of God can even heal our memories to the point that they are no longer painful. He turns sin's wounds into scars that remind us of the sin; but the pain of the past will be gone.

3. <u>Watch</u>

To watch means to be on the alert like a soldier standing guard against a sneak attack of the enemy. Genuine repentance always moves one to watchfulness against possible repetition of the sin.[206] All of us stumble and fall, repeatedly in some things. But God wants us to keep growing. Experience is not what happens to us. Experience is what we learn from what happens to us. We must learn from our experiences so that we don't keep stumbling over the same thing - time after time after time after time. He turns away from the sin. He doesn't keep on doing it and merely saying, "I'm sorry." Belief should determine

---

[202] See Psalm 51.

[203] Psalm 32:1, 2

[204] See Revelation 12:10.

[205] See Jeremiah 31:34

[206] See Mark 14:37, 38; See also Luke 12:15; Acts 20:28; 1Timothy 4:16.

behavior. We cannot talk ourselves out of something we have behaved ourselves into. The Apostle James tells us:

> *What does it profit, my brethren, if someone says he has faith but does not have works? Can faith save him? If a brother or sister is naked and destitute of daily food, and one of you says to them, "Depart in peace, be warmed and filled," but you do not give them the things which are needed for the body, what does it profit? Thus also faith by itself, if it does not have works, is dead. But someone will say, "You have faith, and I have works." Show me your faith without your works, and I will show you my faith by my works. You believe that there is one God. You do well. Even the demons believe--and tremble! But do you want to know, O foolish man, that faith without works is dead? Was not Abraham our father justified by works when he offered Isaac his son on the altar? Do you see that faith was working together with his works, and by works faith was made perfect? And the Scripture was fulfilled which says, "Abraham believed God, and it was accounted to him for righteousness." And he was called the friend of God. You see then that a man is justified by works, and not by faith only. Likewise, was not Rahab the harlot also justified by works when she received the messengers and sent them out another way? For as the body without the spirit is dead, so faith without works is dead also.*[207]

This is not to say that we are saved by faith plus works; but it is saying that the faith that saves always shows itself

---

[207] James 2:14-26

through works. The Hebrew language has no word for faith in the abstract. True faith produces faithfulness.

Periodic Extraordinary Prayer

Periodic extraordinary prayer is essential to regaining and maintaining spiritual vigor both individually and corporately. In the thirteen years I served as associate pastor at Coral Ridge Presbyterian Church, we began every year with a week of daily prayer from five to seven in the morning. ChristChurch in Atlanta, my present home church, begins each year with emphasis on extraordinary prayer.

Church leaders should call their congregations to times of special prayer and fasting so that the church can better understand what it means to be the people of God and to faithfully continue Christ's mission. If you are a leader in your local church, let me urge you to challenge the other leaders to schedule a special week devoted to prayer throughout your congregation. This declares your total dependence on God for all things. As you ask the Lord to provide what your church needs to be His people and faithfully continuing Christ's mission in the coming year, you will find Him "*able to do exceedingly abundantly above all that we ask or think, according to the power that works in us*" (Ephes. 3:20).

At my home church, we urge each member to join with other members and friends in the church community in adding ten minutes daily to their present prayer time. During this time, we read assigned Scripture such as that found in Appendix Three. We meditate on this Scripture and use this meditation as the basis for our prayer. We pray for ourselves, our families, and then two other specific people or families in our local church. We use our Church

Directory to select the two other members or friends. This we do by finding our name and then selecting the next two people in the directory. We ask the Lord to make it very clear which spiritual gifts He has given to us and those for whom we pray. We ask Him to enable us and them to properly use these gifts in His Church.

We pray that the Holy Spirit will build our local church into a more healthy body. And we believe that this vitality will show itself in a healthy interdependence of leaders and workers; of individuals and groups (cell [chain of encouragement[208]], congregation, and celebrating assembly). True spiritual vitality will draw the young and old together,[209] and it will create a dynamic relationship between the local church and home--family and the church as family, resulting in multiplication of new Christians and new congregations.

Spying Out the Land

In addition to consistent prayer for all present laborers church leaders need to "*spy out the land.*"[210] That is, study the neighborhood in which the congregation meets and where its people live and work. In a previous book, we dealt with Old Testament holy war as the basis for New Testament spiritual warfare.[211] To avoid wasting the

---

208 Cf. Archie Parrish, *Improve Your Prayer Life*, pages 59-60 and The Kingdom Campaign, a free sixteen-page booklet available from Serve International.

209 "And he will turn the hearts of the fathers to the children, and the hearts of the children to their fathers, lest I come and strike the earth with a curse" (Malachi 4:6).

210 Numbers 13:2

211 See *Improve Your Prayer Life,* Serve International, Atlanta, 2000, pp. 33-46.

church's vigor, leaders need to develop a strategy sufficient to conquer and occupy their entire territory. In this regard, there are some practical insights to be gained from Israels initial invasion of Palestine.

First, strategy must be designed with proper intelligence on the target area. God commanded Moses to send twelve men to "spy out" the Promised Land. They were charged to "*see what the land is like: whether the people who dwell in it are strong or weak, few or many; whether the land they dwell in is good or bad; whether the cities they inhabit are like camps or strongholds; whether the land is rich or poor; and whether there are forests there or not.*"[212]

Second, the task must be seen in relation to the resources available to conquer and occupy.
On their return, the twelve reported,

> *"We went to the land where you sent us. It truly flows with milk and honey, and this is its fruit. Nevertheless the people who dwell in the land are strong; the cities are fortified and very large; moreover we saw the descendants of Anak there. The Amalekites dwell in the land of the South; the Hittites, the Jebusites, and the Amorites dwell in the mountains; and the Canaanites dwell by the sea and along the banks of the Jordan."*

The people panicked! Then Caleb quieted the people before Moses, and said, "*Let us go up at once and take possession, for we are well able to overcome it.*" But the men who had gone up with him said,

---

212 Numbers 13:18-19

> *"We are not able to go up against the people, for they are stronger than we." And they gave the children of Israel a bad report of the land which they had spied out, saying, "The land through which we have gone as spies is a land that devours its inhabitants, and all the people whom we saw in it are men of great stature. There we saw the giants (the descendants of Anak came from the giants); and we were like grasshoppers in our own sight, and so we were in their sight"*[213]

The challenging task of conquering the Promised Land overwhelmed all the Israelites, except Moses, Aaron, Joshua and Caleb. The mob moaned that they would all die and their children would become prisoners of war. They cried out for a new leader to take them back to Egypt. Their eyes were so fixed on the problems of conquest that they could not see the greatness of their God. Moses' intercession resulted in the people being saved from annihilation and only being sentenced to forty years wandering in the wilderness, one year for each day of the spy expedition. Only when the adults died, were their children allowed to enter the land.[214] Finally, forty years later when the next generation entered Palestine, Joshua divided the land among the tribes and gave them the responsibility to conquer their portion.[215]

Spying out your "Promised Land" will clear the fog from your "harvest field" and allow you to see opportunities for

---

[213] Numbers 13:27-33

[214] See Numbers 14:1-45

[215] Numbers 34:13-15

ministry. Once the opportunities are identified, you can divide the campaign into manageable tasks. Identifying the specific tasks will enable you to know the gifts and talents needed to bring in the harvest. Then ask the Lord of Harvest to provide these workers.

Like the Apostles, begin by joining together in extraordinary prayer. Each believer already has three spheres of activity: where you corporately worship, where you as an individual live and where you work. God, in His wise providence, places churches and people where He can best use them for His glory. Therefore, local churches are responsible for the people living in a reasonable radius of the building where they gather. From a practical standpoint, local churches should intentionally plan to minister as God enables to every person within a Sunday-morning thirty-minute drive of their corporate meeting place.

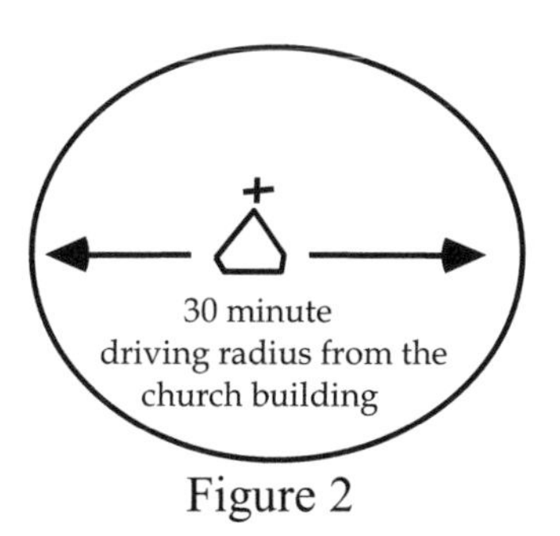

Figure 2

Furthermore, individual Christians are responsible to minister to the people in their circles of influence, especially their neighbors and work associates.[216] Believers should see their homes as outposts of heaven, centers for

---

216 See *Impact Your World,* "Relationship Review," pages 168-171.

ministry to the people around them.[217] God gives gifts to His people and guides them in the investment of these gifts. Therefore, the workplace is much more than a place to earn a paycheck.

One additional thought on "spying out the land," Don't let your analysis of your "Promised Land" move you to terrified paralysis. There are "giants in the land." But keep your eyes on your Sovereign Lord and trust Him to defeat the foes. This spiritual battle is the Lord's!

Structural Renewal

To regain vigor we must work on structural renewal in our personal walk with Christ and within each local church. This requires the formation and strengthening of nuclear subcommunities within the larger church community. Loveless puts it this way, "Vitality in the church of Christ gathers around centered groups of Christians who are interacting with one another and with other groups, like organs in a body. The most natural microcommunity in the church is the Christian home and pastors should work to build up this unit into the functional strength it enjoyed in Puritanism [or in the patriarchal household in the Bible, which was the Puritan model].[218]

History shows that renewal never takes hold unless it is embodied, exemplified, lived out by a particular group, who show the way to a stronger faith by taking it

---

217 See Archie Parrish, "Appendix Three, A Room-by-Room Review," *Intercede For and With Your Family*, Serve International, Atlanta, GA p. 145-162. This exercise provides direction on transforming your home into an outpost of heaven.

218 Loveless, *Dynamics of Spiritual Life,* p. 226. See also *Intercede for and with Your Family,*

themselves. History also reveals that lifting the level of people's commitment to meaning is the hardest work there is, and there is no shortcut or gimmick that will make it any easier, whether inside or outside the existing churches. What costs little, accomplishes little. The greater the effect desired, the greater the effort required to achieve it. And there is no effect greater than the enlistment of men in the service of saving souls.

To regain vigor we should utilize the strategy of the little church in the big church. Little churches within the church (the *ecclesiolae* in *ecclesia*) have infused new vigor and resilience into local churches throughout the centuries. The little churches *(ecclesiola)* served as a legitimated but not subservient source of encouragement, example, criticism, goading, and competition to the rest of the church. It raised the general level of demand and commitment by its own greater strictness (an injection of new stringency rather than an imposition of stricture), but it also felt the equal and opposite reaction of the resistant environing mass.[219]

Strictness Is Important

Dean Kelley reports that, "An examination of religious movements and innovative communities suggest that social strength will not be retained without strictness, and that once strictness has ebbed away (taking with it strength), it is difficult if not impossible to recover. If this is the case, it is not because strictness cannot be newly conceptualized or formulated in regulations, but because it is virtually impossible to apply or enforce in an existing organization. People who have become accustomed to leniency do not find it congenial to contemplate strictness, let alone live under it. Yet--if this analysis is correct--strictness is the

---

[219] Dean Kelley, *Why Conservative Churches are Growing, A Study in Sociology of Religion*, Harper & Row, New York, 1972, pp. 114-116.

only way to conserve social strength, whether in *ecclesia* or *ecclesiolae.*"[220]

Kelley expands this thought: "The indispensability of strictness seems to some an ungracious and abrasive prescription, if not incomprehensible. Yet it is simply the necessary corollary and projection of seriousness in what one is doing. Soren Kierkegaard calls it 'severity, the severity which is inseparable from the seriousness of eternity.'[221] If one is dealing with matters of salvation, of eternity, then it makes a vast difference whether one does what is 'right' or its opposite. As religious groups age and mellow, they tend to relax their severity, their strictness, their seriousness. Kierkegaard's *Attack upon Christendom* is a vehement denunciation of the state church of Denmark for its lack of seriousness, or rather, its insistence that seriousness is not necessary to Christianity, which is thereby allowed to degenerate into a smug paganism in which things are called Christian without having to be any different from what they were: 'What Christianity wanted was earnestness in living, and to do away with vain honors and glories, [but] everything remained as it was, the change being that it assumed the predicate 'christian': the gewgaws of knightly orders, titles, rank, etc. became 'Christian'--and the priest is tickled to death when he himself is decorated with--the cross. The Cross! Yes, in the Christianity of 'Christendom' the Cross has become something like the child's hobby-horse and trumpet."[222]

---

220 Ibid., 119-120.

221 Soren Kierkegaard, *Attack upon Christendom* (Boston: Beacon Press, 1956), p. 123.

222 Kelley, *Why Conservative Churches are Growing, A Study in Sociology of Religion*, pp, 164-5.

Jesus taught us to pray, "Thy Kingdom come!" which implies that prayer is the main instrument through which the kingdom of God can be understood and advanced by church members. Therefore, it is important that members be involved in some prayer center whose vision is comprehensive. This is the reason for the Kingdom Campaign. As the "Chain of Encouragement" is built in local congregations a cellular network of microcommunities is accomplished by an outward restructuring of its awareness and contact with other local churches of various denominations, its own denominational network and the relations of denominations with one another, and the local and national human communities and their needs. This restructuring should produce new systems of communication linking these networks together in productive labor for the advancement of the kingdom. This must begin with concerned corporate prayer.

Work Must be Divided and Delegated[223]

When God brought the Israelites into the Promised Land, He told Joshua to divide the land among the twelve tribes. Then each tribe was responsible for conquering and occupying its own territory. But a strange thing happened to the Israelites. Once they had conquered enough land for their immediate use, they stopped fighting. Men of war laid down the sword and took up the plow and sickle. The fiery-eyed fighters from the desert became the well-fed farmers of a land flowing with milk and honey.

God was not happy with the Israelites' failure to occupy the *whole* Promised Land. In fact much of Israel's trouble

---

223 This is more fully developed in "The Joshua Predicament," David A Womack, *The Pyramid Principle of Church Growth, Bethany Fellowship,* Minneapolis, MN, 1977, pages 13-24.

since that time have resulted from failure to obey fully God's command to drive the enemy out of the land. "When Joshua was old and well advanced in years, the LORD said to him, '*You are very old, and there are still very large areas of land to be taken over.*' "[224] Joshua's predicament was that he ran out of time and momentum before he finished his God-given task. The Lord demanded the total occupation of the Promised Land, not just a token presence; but the leaders were old and tired and ready to settle down short of fulfilling their destiny.

Today, we face the problem of aging leaders, a casual church, and an unfinished task. Many of the growing problems of our day are the result of the American Christians settling for "token presence" rather than total conquest. We cocoon in our homes like our fearful pagan neighbors while godless predators prowl our streets. To obey our God, to capture our cities for righteousness, we must get out of our cocoons and into the streets.

The accomplishing of God's work through our local church does not require the cooperative effort of *all* members of our congregations. But it does require a supercritical mass of Kingdom Intercessors—improving their own prayer life, interceding for and with their families, invigorating their churches, and impacting their world. And rather than merely preaching and exhorting people to this end, leaders should encourage and equip Kingdom Intercessors in fireteams and build the Chain of Encouragement.

In hundreds of cities across North America and around the globe, ordinary believers have made their homes into

---

[224] Joshua 13:1

"Lighthouses of prayer"[225] and have regular routines of PrayerWalking through the streets of their neighborhood. They pray while walking, with eyes watching for the spiritual awakening they ask God to bring.

PrayerWalking is going on-site to gain insight for intercession. There is no one PrayerWalking formula. PrayerWalkers engage in every imaginable style. There is nothing magic in the footsteps. God's Spirit is simply helping us to pray with persistent spontaneity in the midst of the very settings we expect him to answer our prayers. Getting up close to the community focuses and sharpens our prayers by concentrating on specific homes and families.

Our praying is enlarged as we cry out for entire communities to know God's healing presence. Pray with disciplined regularity in fireteams,[226] pairs, and small bands. Thus PrayerWalkers keep near their neighbors in order to touch their city with the gospel's transforming power. Quiet triumphs follow as God changes our city day-by-day and house-by-house.[227]

Dean Kelley cautions, "The propensity of little bands of men and women to set up a new way of life together is

---

[225] Lighthouse Movement—www.lighthousemovement.com. See also Prayer Walking Video by Ted Haggard, New Life Church, supplied by Mission America.

[226] See *Improve Your Prayer Life, "Fireteams,"* pp. 113-118.

[227] Steve Hawthorne and Graham Kendrick, *Prayerwalking, Praying on Site with Insight*, Creation House, Orlando, 1993. Also check out the extensive resources listed by Mission America, 5666 Lincoln Drive, Suite 100, Minneapolis, MN 55436, Phone (952) 912-0001 or on the internet at http://www.missionamerica.org/

equaled only by their inability to keep it going."[228] In the next chapter we will consider how to maintain spiritual vigor in our personal lives and in the congregation.

---

228 Kelley, *Why Conservative Churches are Growing, A Study in Sociology of Religion*, p. 116.

How Does a Church Maintain Vigor?

Maintaining the spiritual vigor to be the people of God, faithfully continuing Christ's mission requires consistent, loving obedient use of means God has provided: prayer and the ministry of the word.[229] Satan has always sought to lure God's people to rely on means other than those provided by God. Israel frequently made alliance with godless nations to "insure" their ability to defeat menacing enemies. Today many churches are using human substitutes for the divine means of grace.[230] The corporate paradigm is the dominant model of our day. Many business people have concluded that the church's lack of effectiveness stems from its inefficient management and lack of planning.

In the infant apostolic church a conflict arose over the question of more aid being given to one group of widows than to another. The Apostles saw this conflict as a potential drain of the church's vigor. To them the question was not, is it important to care for widows?. The issue was rather what had God called them, as apostles, to do. Scripture records, "*Then the twelve summoned the multitude of the disciples and said, 'It is not desirable that we should leave the word of God and serve tables. Therefore, brethren, seek out from among you seven men of good reputation, full of the Holy Spirit and wisdom, whom we may appoint over this business; but we will give*

---

[229] For discussion of an individual's maintenance of spiritual vigor, see "Loving Obedience—the Key to Increased Power in Prayer" (pages 80-88) and "Growth Cycle" (pages 89-92), Archie Parrish, *Improve Your Prayer Life.*

[230] See Ian Murray, *Evangelicalism Divided, a Record of Crucial Change in the Years 1950-2000*, Banner of Truth Trust, Edinburgh, 2000.

ourselves continually to prayer and to the ministry of the word.'"

Prayer and the Ministry of the Word

Scripture declares, "*The word of God is living and powerful, and sharper than any two-edged sword, piercing even to the division of soul and spirit, and of joints and marrow, and is a discerner of the thoughts and intents of the heart.*"[231] God's people are "*born again, not of corruptible seed but incorruptible, through the word of God which lives and abides forever.*"[232] Congregational vitality is dependent on anointed, powerful preaching and teaching of God's word. And God has designed the ministry of the Word in such a way that it will not have full power and authority unless it is joined with biblical prayer. Jesus said, "*If you abide in Me, and My words abide in you, you will ask what you desire, and it shall be done for you.*"[233] God uniquely blesses the balanced blend of prayer and the word. This blessing is never automatic or mechanical; it is always God's sovereign, wise, gracious choice. He regenerates the soul and then the soul turns in saving faith to the Savior.

The sun shines its life-giving rays on the barren desert but the desert remains a wasteland. The same sun's vital influences fall on a fertile plain. It is clothed with all the wonders of vegetation and beauty. The high-noon brilliance of the sun does not penetrate the midnight darkness of blind eyes. It is similar with spiritual truth. No matter what may be its intrinsic power, it has no helpful effect unless the

---

[231] Hebrews 4:12

[232] 1 Peter 1:23

[233] John 15:7

mind to which it is presented is quickened to receive it. Without God's granting of what Jonathan Edwards called, "a divine and supernatural life,"[234] the minds of men and women are not able to receive the transforming and saving power of the truths of the Bible.[235] Therefore, for the word of God to produce salvation it must be preceded and attended by the supernatural power of the Holy Spirit, and for this quickening of the soul we must prayerfully plead.[236]

God has ordained prayer and the word to be the *ordinary channels* of His grace, *i.e.*, of the supernatural influences of the Holy Spirit, to human souls.[237] The writer of the book of Hebrews tells us, *"We do not have a High Priest who cannot sympathize with our weaknesses, but was in all points tempted as we are, yet without sin. Let us therefore come boldly to the throne of grace, that we may obtain mercy and find grace to help in time of need."*[238] Here God promises that in time of need, bold prayer will obtain mercy and grace to help. Here God indicates He has ordained prayer to communicate the life-giving and sanctifying influences of the Spirit to human souls. When a quickened soul draws near to God, God draws near to it[239], manifests His glory, sheds abroad His love[240], and imparts

---

234 Jonathan Edwards, "The Divine and Supernatural Light," in *The Works of Jonathan Edwards*, Volume 2, Banner of Truth Trust, Edinburgh, 1974. This message was used by God to begin the First Great Awakening in America in 1738.

235 See John 8:43, 47.

236 See 1 Corinthians 2:14. Robert L. Dabney provides additional insight on this thought. See his *Lectures in Systematic Theology,* Zondervan, Grand Rapids, First printed 1878. Reprint Edition 1972, pp. 472-473.

237 This truth is covered in more detail in Charles Hodge, *Systematic Theology* Vol III, p. 406.

238 Hebrews 4:15-16

239 James 4:8

240 Romans 5:5

that peace which passes all understanding. In other words, prayer is a usual and necessary means for all gracious growth. Robert Dabney enlarges on this important truth:

> Faith is a mother grace for all others; but prayer is the natural and necessary expression of faith; it is its language, its vital breath. In spiritual desire the life of religion may be said to consist. Desire is implied in faith itself, for people do not trust for what they do not want, and it is yet more manifest in hope, for hope is but desire encouraged by the prospect of obtaining the desired object. Repentance includes a desire for deliverance from sin and attainment of holiness. Love of God includes a desire for communion with Him and for His favor. So that it would be accurate to say that practical religion consists in the exercise of holy desires.
>
> But what is prayer, except "an offering up of our desires to God?"[241] Prayer is the vital breath of religion in the soul. Again it cultivates our sense of dependence and of God's sovereignty. By confessing our sins, the sense of sin is deepened. By rendering thanks, gratitude is enlivened. By adoring the divine perfections, we are changed into the same image, from glory to glory.
>
> From all this it is apparent that prayer is the Christian's vital breath. If God had not required it,

---

241 *Westminster Shorter Catechism* Q. 98. What is prayer? A. Prayer is an offering up of our desires unto God for things agreeable to His will in the name of Christ with confession of our sins and thankful acknowledgment of His mercies.

> the Christian would be compelled to offer it by his own irrepressible promptings. If he were taught to believe that it was not only useless, but wrong, he would doubtless offer it in his heart in spite of himself, even though he were obliged to accompany it with a petition that God would forgive the offering. To have no prayer is, for human beings to have no religion.
>
> But last, and chiefly, prayer is a means of grace, because God has appointed it as the instrument of man's receiving His spiritual influences. It is enough for the Christian to know that all his growth in grace is dependent, and that God has ordained: "*everyone who asks receives*."[242]

Prayer has the relation that any other cause has to the end for which it was appointed. Therefore, it is the condition on which the blessings of God are given. But prayer also brings us near to God, and intimacy with Him moves us to exercise gracious affections and reverence.

One of the most strategic issues for church vigor is prayer. Leaders and workers of the local church must be people of prayer and they must be prayed for. We will consider this matter in the next chapter.

---

242 Matthew 7:7-8. Also see Robert L. Dabney, *Lectures in Systematic Theology,* Zondervan, Grand Rapids, First printed 1878. Reprint Edition 1972 pp. 716-717.

Armorbearers Intercessors Ministry

Wilson stepped to his pulpit; words came slowly and with great emotion. "I wish I had started my ministry this way!" Standing before Wilson more than 400 members of the Kirk of the Hills indicating that, for the next year, they would pray for him and his family at each meal. Kirk of the Hills is one of the growing army of local churches where the pastors are the chief prayer warriors and the congregations are their Armorbearers. As a warrior chief depended on his armorbearers to raise their shields to ward off the enemy arrows, so Church leaders depend on their people's prayers to protect them from the "flaming arrows" of the evil one.[243]

Armorbearer Intercessor's Ministry is a spiritual advance that is achieved by increased leadership effectiveness and congregational unity resulting from regular focused prayer of members for their leaders and workers.

"There is nothing that makes us love a man so much as praying for him."
William Law

<u>The Warrior Chief</u>

In ancient times, men became kings by leading their troops to victory over opposing armies. Therefore, warrior chiefs were always strategic targets for the enemy. If the chief were killed, his army would usually lose heart and be routed.[244] Sometimes a single armorbearer went to battle in front of his chief. He carried a large shield to protect his

243 Ephesians 6: 16

244 See 1 Kings 22:29-36

chief. Jonathan and his armorbearer are an example of this.[245] During Roman times, some warrior chiefs recruited their most proven, valiant, devoted soldiers to be armorbearers in a formation called the "turtle phalanx" because it resembled a giant turtle moving across the battlefield. An inner circle surrounded the chief and lifted their shields above their heads to form a roof. An outer circle formed a protective wall around the whole squad. They pressed close together, shields interlocked.

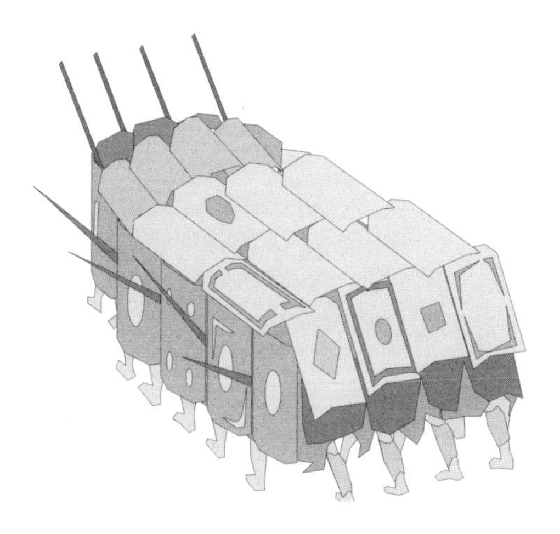

Armorbearers and their proper use of shields were important for military victory. Shields are a defensive armament held by hand or attached to the arm to ward of blows or projectiles. Shields were decorated with tribal or personal emblems and from this developed the art of heraldry and blazonry that still exists today. The buckler, target, and targe were small shields used to ward off blows in hand-to-hand combat. The pavis shield was large and rectangular like a door. It was used to defend against archery. A soldier's whole body could be concealed behind

---

245 See 1 Samuel 14:6-14

this shield, which was made from wood or wickerwork overlaid with leather. The leather was oiled before battle to preserve and make it glisten. The oil also made the surface slippery. In battle it sometimes had a red appearance either because it was dyed red or overlaid with burnished copper. These pavis door-sized shields, used in the "turtle phalanx" formation, provided a protective wall for the warrior chief. He could lead his army and still have a degree of safety.

The visible leaders of the local church (especially the pastors) are strategic targets for the devil. Jesus makes this clear.[246] During the last supper, Jesus warned the Twelve that before the night passed they would all fall away because of Him. Peter boasted his loyalty, "*Lord, I am ready to go with you to prison and to death.*" To Peter, Jesus answered, "*I tell you, Peter, before the rooster crows today, you will deny three times that you know me.*"

Jesus parts the curtain between time and eternity and tells us two significant truths. First, he tells us that Satan preys on leaders. Jesus said, "*Simon, Simon, Satan has asked to sift you as wheat.*"[247] Satan existed before time began. He was the highest created angelic being. Originally he was called Lucifer, Son of the Morning, but he was lifted up with pride in his own heart and was cast out of Heaven, taking with him one-third of the angels.[248] These disobedient angels fell from their high, holy position and became demonic. Lucifer became Satan or the devil. He is a created, spirit being. He is not greater than nor equal with God, but he is more powerful and wiser than man. Because he is a spirit being, he never needs to take time to eat or

---

246 See Luke 22: 31-34

247 Luke 22:31

248 See Isaiah 14:12-15 and Revelation 12:4

sleep. Because God pronounced judgment upon Satan, he hates God and seeks to strike at Him in every way that he possibly can. Since Satan is a created being, he can only do what God allows and that only for as long as God allows.

God made the original man and woman in His own image and gave them dominion over the earth. When they yielded to the temptation of the devil, they lost this power of dominion to the evil one. This is why Satan is called the "*god of this age*."[249] Now Satan seeks in every way he possibly can to destroy the people of God. He is called the "*accuser of the brothers*."[250] Sometimes he viciously attacks as a "*roaring lion*."[251] Other times he subtly inserts himself as a lying, hissing "*serpent*"[252], but he is most dangerous when he appears as an "*angel of light*."[253] Jesus declared that he was a liar from the beginning and a murderer.[254]

Satan is a defeated foe. When Satan seduced Adam and Eve, God promised, "*I will put enmity between you and the woman, and between your seed and her Seed; he shall bruise your head, and you shall bruise His heel*."[255] The Apostle John explains, "*For this purpose the Son of God was manifested, that He might destroy the works of the devil*."[256] On the cross, the decisive battle in the war between Christ and the devil was won; therefore, the devil is not an ultimate threat to believers. Remember, "You are

---

249 2 Corinthians 4:4

250 Revelation 12:10

251 1 Peter 5:8

252 Genesis 3:1

253 2 Corinthians 11:14

254 John 8:44

255 Genesis 3:15

256 1 John 3:8

of God, little children, and have overcome them, because He who is in you is greater than he who is in the world."[257]

It appears from the statement, "Satan has *asked*," that even Satan prays to God. Never does he praise or thank God, nor does he ever confess his sin. When Satan prays, he seeks to gain God's permission, for without it he can do nothing. When Jesus said, "Satan has asked for *you,*" the plural pronoun is used. Satan asked for the Twelve. Satan has spent thousands of years studying human beings. He seeks to destroy all believers. But since he is limited in what he can do, he strategically concentrates on leaders. When he destroys a leader, this makes an impact on all the followers.

Luke tells us that Satan asked to sift the Twelve as wheat. Notice that Satan did not ask to *kill* the Twelve, which would have made martyrs of them. In the course of time, all the apostles except John did seal their testimony with their blood. But now Satan asks to *sift them as wheat.* Before wheat is edible, the husk must be separated from the grain. In ancient times this was accomplished by bringing the wheat to the threshing floor. Workers would use giant fan-shaped implements to scoop up the wheat and toss it in the air. The wind would blow the light husk away and the heavier wheat would fall to the floor. This is a picture of what Satan desires to do to the Twelve. He wants to stress them out! He wanted to make them unstable and leave them in positions of responsibility. Wherever he can, Satan seeks to deceive, disgrace and *then* destroy. Judas is a classic example of this tactic. Under Satan's influence, Judas sold his Lord for thirty pieces of silver and then hanged himself. Any professed believer who puts money

---

[257] 1 John 4:4

above Christ is a descendant of Judas. Satan desires Judas' fate for all Christian leaders.

Wherever he can, Satan seeks to deceive, disgrace and *then* destroy.

Why did God grant Satan permission to *sift*[258] the Twelve? Chaff must be sifted from the wheat before the wheat can be made into bread. Self-reliance must be sifted from the Twelve before God can use them to the full. God uses even the devil to purge sin from His people.

Satan directed his full force against the Apostles. They were the leaders of the infant Christian church. Destroy them and he could destroy the whole human race! Today he still seeks to destroy church leaders because through them he brings the greatest devastation on the church and the world.

Peter suffered Satan's sifting and he warns believers, "*Be sober, be vigilant; because your adversary the devil walks about like a roaring lion, seeking whom he may devour. Resist him, steadfast in the faith, knowing that the same sufferings are experienced by your brotherhood in the world.*"[259] According to Peter, when God allows Satan to sift His people, we should not passively submit.[260]

---

258 The NASV translates this, "Satan "has demanded permission." We need to underscore what we have said earlier in this book, where Christians are willfully inconsistent in what they say they believe and how they behave, where this gap exists, God may allow Satan to sift. Even the Apostle Paul was given a thorn in the flesh, a messenger of Satan" to keep him humble.

259 1 Peter 5:8-9 See also James 4:7

260 Abraham Kuyper, *The Practice of Godliness,* Baker Book House, Grand Rapids, MI, n.d.

The second significant truth we learn from this text is that Jesus prays for leaders. *"I have prayed for you, Simon, that your faith may not fail. And when you have turned back, strengthen your brothers."*[261]

Here we see intercession in its purist form. In all intercession at least three persons must always be concerned: the one who speaks, the one spoken to, and the one spoken for or against. In this situation, Jesus speaks to the Father for Peter. Also at least three things must always be presumed: need, on the part of the one spoken of; power, on the part of the one spoken to; and contact with both these persons on the part of the one who speaks. Peter needed divine grace to preserve him through Satan's sifting. The Father had the power and Jesus had contact with Peter and the Father. Richard Sibbes, warns, "When we go to God by prayer, the devil knows we go to fetch strength against him, and, therefore, he opposes us all he can."[262]

Jesus prayed with sharp focus. He interceded by name, "Simon." He used Peter's old name because He knew that Peter's old nature was rearing up again. Judas betrayed his Lord and then committed suicide. Peter denied his Lord and then became the leading Apostle in the early church. A basic difference between the two is Jesus prayed for Peter, but He did not pray for Judas.

Jesus at this point focused His intercession on Peter and not the rest of the disciples. Simon was the most visible of all the leaders of the embryonic Christian Church. In the four

---

[261] Luke 22:31-32

[262] Richard Sibbs, *Divine Meditations,* Banner of Truth Trust, Edinburgh, 1973, p. 164.

lists of the Twelve, Peter is always first. Most of the time Peter is the spokesman for the Twelve and had great influence over them.

In the book of Revelation, Jesus holds seven stars in His right hand and He explains that, "*The seven stars are the angels of the seven churches*."[263] The Greek word *angelos,* translated here as angel, refers to the pastors of the seven churches. From this we may conclude that Jesus holds pastors with His mighty right hand.

Jesus lives forever to make intercession. When the forty days of our Lord's risen life on earth were ended, *"He led them out as far as Bethany, and He lifted up His hands and blessed them. Now it came to pass, while He blessed them, that He was parted from them and carried up into heaven."*[264] This farewell benediction was the signal of the Redeemer's entrance on His ministry of intercession. The nail-pierced hands, lifted over the bowed heads of the disciples, are to us the symbol of His unchangeable priesthood, and the assurance that He ever lives to make intercession for us.

The heavenly ministry of Christ was foreshadowed in His High-Priestly Prayer. The words "I pray" do not simply mean entreaty, but a request as between equals, and this idea is strengthened by the use of the phrase "I will."[265] Our Lord is no longer the lowly suppliant of earth, wearing the servant's girdle, and perfecting His obedience even unto death,[266] but the Man who is Jehovah's Fellow. He

---

263 Revelation 1:20

264 Luke 24: 50-5I

265 See John 17: 9, I5, 20, 24

266 See Philippians 2:7-8

intercedes from the throne. He offers His requests in the power of an accepted sacrifice. He asks for that purchased possession which is His by right.[267]

Jesus prayed with great confidence. He assumes that His prayer will be answered: *"And when you have turned back, strengthen your brothers."*[268] Christ's intercession was effective. Peter, like the prodigal, did come to his senses. He was in the prayer meeting with the 120 in the opening chapter of the book of Acts. And when he preached on Pentecost, 3,000 came to faith in Jesus as the Messiah.[269] Peter also wrote two epistles to strengthen his brothers. The incident of Satan's sifting and Jesus' intercession must have been in Peter's mind when he wrote 1 Pet. 5:6-11.

> *Therefore humble yourselves under the mighty hand of God, that He may exalt you in due time, casting all your care upon Him, for He cares for you. Be sober, be vigilant; because your adversary the devil walks about like a roaring lion, seeking whom he may devour. Resist him, steadfast in the faith, knowing that the same sufferings are experienced by your brotherhood in the world. But may the God of all grace, who called us to His eternal glory by Christ Jesus, after you have suffered a while, perfect, establish, strengthen, and settle you. To Him be the glory and the dominion forever and ever. Amen.*

---

267 D. M. M'Intyre, *The Prayer Life of Our Lord Morgan & Scott,* London, n.d. pp. 143-147, describes the intercession of Christ for His people.

268 Luke 22:32

269 See Acts 2:14:16

Since Satan preys on leaders and Jesus prays for leaders, then leaders must be people of prayer and they must be prayed for. Jesus commanded His disciples to "Watch and pray so that you will not fall into temptation" (Matt. 26:41; Mark 14:38). All leaders, not merely those in the local church, if they are in politics, business, or any other legitimate endeavor, should be people of prayer. But church leaders should model the place of prayer in leadership responsibilities that shows all other Christian leaders how to pray in the areas where God has called them. The pastor is the key spiritual leader of the church's spiritual leaders. Charles Spurgeon eloquently speaks to the necessity of the pastor's private prayer.

> Above all others, the preacher is distinguished as a man of prayer. He prays as much as an ordinary Christian, else he were a hypocrite. He prays more than ordinary Christians, else he is disqualified for the office that he has undertaken ....The prayer closet is the best study. The commentators are good instructors, but the Author himself is far better, and prayer makes a direct appeal to him and enlists him in our cause... If we cannot prevail with men for God, we will, at least, endeavor to prevail with God for men.... Great talents you may never have, but you will do well enough without them if you abound in intercession.... The minister who does not earnestly pray over his work must surely be a vain and conceited man. He acts as if he thought himself sufficient of himself, and therefore needed not to appeal to God.... The preacher who neglects to pray much must be a mere official, tempted into a pulpit because the piece of bread which belongs to the priest's office is very necessary to him, or a detestable hypocrite who loves the praise of men,

> and cares not for the praise of God.... The preacher who neglects to pray much will surely become a mere superficial talker, best approved where grace is least valued and a vain show most admired. He cannot be one of those who plow deep and reap abundant harvests. He is a mere loiterer, not a laborer. As a preacher he has a name to live and is dead.... We not only ought to pray more, but we must. The fact is, the secret of all ministerial success lies in prevalence at the mercy seat.[270]

Soon I will celebrate forty years as an ordained pastor but only recently have I come to see the difference between praying to live the Christian life and living the Christian life to pray. And I am greatly saddened by the reality that most of my comrades in the pulpit today have yet to come to this realization. God graciously, patiently dealt with me for more than thirty years to bring me to this awareness so I recognize the need for longsuffering to others, but we preachers and the church are missing so much because of our prayerlessness.

Soon I will celebrate forty years as an ordained pastor but only recently have I come to see the difference between praying to live the Christian life and living the Christian life to pray.

P. T. Forsyth admonished, "The pride of learning is against the dependent humility of prayer. Prayer is with the pulpit too often only official — a performance for the routine of service. Prayer is not to the modern pulpit the mighty force

---

270 Charles Spurgeon, "The Preacher's Private Prayer," *Lectures To My Students,* Pilgrim Press, Pasadena, TX, 1990, pp. 40-52.

it was in Paul's life or Paul's ministry. Every preacher who does not make prayer a mighty factor in his own life and ministry is himself weak as a factor in God's work and is powerless to project God's cause in this world"

Forsyth continues, "The preacher may feel from the kindling of his own sparks, be eloquent over his own exegesis, earnest in delivering the product of his own brain; the professor may usurp the place and imitate the fire of the apostle; brains and nerves may serve the place and feign the work of God's Spirit, and by these forces the letter may glow and sparkle like an illumined text, but the glow and sparkle will be as barren of life as the field sown with pearls. The death-dealing element lies back of the words, back of the sermon, back of the occasion, back of the manner, back of the action. The great hindrance is in the preacher himself. He has not in himself the mighty life-creating forces. There may be no discount on his orthodoxy, honesty, cleanness, or earnestness; but somehow the man, the inner man, in its secret places has never broken down and surrendered to God, his inner life is not a great highway for the transmission of God's message, God's power. Somehow self and not God rules in the holy of holies. Somewhere, all unconscious to himself, some spiritual nonconductor has touched his inner being, and the divine current.

"His inner being has never felt its thorough spiritual bankruptcy, its utter powerlessness; he has never learned to cry out with an ineffable cry of self-despair and self-helplessness till God's power and God's fire comes in and fills, purifies, empowers. Self-esteem, self-ability in some pernicious shape has defamed and violated the temple, which should be held sacred for God. Life-giving preaching costs the preacher much — death to self, crucifixion to the world, the travail of his own soul. Crucified preaching only can give life. Crucified preaching can come only from a crucified man.

"Prayerless preaching kills! Without prayer the preacher creates death and not life. The preacher who is feeble in prayer is feeble in life-giving forces. The preacher who no longer prays as a conspicuous and prevailing element in his own character has cut the distinctive life-giving power from his preaching. Professional praying there is and will be, but professional praying helps the preaching to its deadly work. Professional praying chills and kills both preaching and praying. Much of the lax devotion and lazy, irreverent attitudes in congregational praying are attributable to professional praying in the pulpit. Long, discursive, dry, and inane are the prayers in many pulpits. Without unction or heart, they fall like a killing frost on all the graces of worship. Death-dealing prayers they are. Every vestige of devotion has perished under their breath. The deader they are the longer they grow. A plea for short praying, live praying, real heart praying, praying by the Holy Spirit — direct, specific, ardent, simple, unctuous in the pulpit — is in order. A school to teach preachers how to pray, as God counts praying, would be more beneficial to true piety, true worship, and true preaching than all theological schools."

Much of the lax devotion and lazy, irreverent attitudes in congregational praying are attributable to professional praying in the pulpit.

Robert Murray McCheyne warns preachers, "If you do not pray, God will probably lay you aside from your ministry as he did me, to teach you to pray. Remember Luther's maxim, 'To have prayed well is to have studied well.'

"Study universal holiness of life. Your whole usefulness depends on this, for your sermons last but an hour or two; your life preaches all the week. If Satan can only make a covetous minister a lover of praise, of pleasure, of good eating, he has ruined your ministry. Give yourself to prayer, and get your texts, your thoughts, your words from God. Luther spent his best three hours in prayer."[271]

Forsyth pleads, "What the Church needs today is not more or better technology, not new organizations or more and novel methods, but men whom the Holy Ghost can use — men of prayer, men mighty in prayer. The Holy Ghost does not flow through methods, but through men. He does not come on technology, but on men. He does not anoint plans, but men — men of prayer.

"The man — God's man — is made in the prayer closet. His life and his profoundest convictions are born in his secret communion with God. The burdened and tearful agony of his spirit, his weightiest and sweetest messages are received when he is alone with God. Prayer makes the man; prayer makes the preacher; prayer makes the pastor."[272]

Therefore, we repeat, church leaders, especially pastors, must be people of prayer! And church members should pray for their leaders, especially their pastor.

---

271 Robert Murray McCheyne, Andrew Alexander Bonar, *Memoir and remains of the Rev. Robert Murray McCheyne, minister of St. Peter's church, Dundee*, Edinburgh: Oliphant, Anderson, 1913.

272 P. T. Forsyth, *The Soul of Prayer,* Eerdmans Publishing, Grand Rapids, MI, 1916, p. 55.
<http://www.ccel.org/f/forsyth/soul_of_prayer/soul_of_prayer.htm>

Do not pray in vague generalities, such as, "Lord, bless my pastor." Vague prayer is the death of prayer. Be specific. Pray for him, his wife and his children *by name.* Pray that he will see himself not as peacetime businessman, but as leader of a wartime guerrilla band engaged in spiritual combat. The world, the flesh and the devil are formidable foes! Men and women apart from Christ are blind. They are captives, bound by the evil one who seeks to destroy them for all eternity![273] Pray that your pastor will live and work each day so that he may be able to stand before the Lord and say, "*I have fought a good fight, I have finished my course, I have kept the faith.*"[274]

In your private devotions, pray that your pastor will have consistent private time with the Lord each day. In your family worship, pray that your pastor will have consistent meaningful prayer time for and with his family. Whenever you eat a meal, ask God to equip your pastor to feed you and the entire flock with the whole council of God. My wife and I have become so anchored to praying for our pastor when we eat, that it has become second nature to intercede for him whether we are alone at home or in public. When someone else says the grace, I quietly pray for our pastor.

In many churches an appointed layperson leads the congregation in prayer for their pastor as part of the Sunday worship. Small groups and Bible classes also should pray for their pastors whenever they meet.

---

273 For fuller explanation of spiritual warfare see *Improve Your Prayer Life.* pp. 33-67. For fuller explanation of the condition of people outside of Christ, see *Impact Your World*, pp. 51-55.

274 2 Timothy 4: 7

Paul was probably the most gifted Christian leader in the history of the church. But he knew that his gifts needed to be empowered by the Holy Spirit for him to be able to do the will of God. So he constantly asked Christians to pray for him (See Appendix Three). If Paul needed prayer support for his gifts to be empowered, how much more do pastors today need their congregation's prayers for their ministry to be empowered?

The pastor sets the pace and the pattern for the congregation.[275] A few members of a congregation may exceed the pastor's godliness, but most will not grow beyond the level modeled by their pastor.[276]

Armorbearers Duties

1. Pray for your pastor and his family at each meal. Someone has suggested the following starting points in praying for your pastor.

Sunday: Favor with God (spiritual revelation, anointing, and holiness).

Monday: Favor with others (congregation, ministry staff, unsaved).

Tuesday: Increased vision (wisdom and enlightenment, motives, guidance).

Wednesday: Spirit, soul, body (health, appearance, attitudes, spiritual and physical wholeness).

Thursday: Protection (temptation, deception, and enemies).

Friday: Finances (priorities, blessings).

Saturday: Family (general, spouse, and children).[277]

---

[275] See 1 Timothy 4:12

[276] See Hosea 4:6-9; Luke 6:40

[277] See C. Peter Wagner, *The Prayer Shield, How to Intercede for Pastors, Christian Leaders & Others on the Spiritual Frontlines,* Regal Books, Ventura, CA, 1997, p. 177, 1992

2. Pray for other leaders one per day on a rotating basis. Intercession should be in relation to the Kingdom of God and the Great Commission.

3. Pray and work for increased demonstration of spiritual unity. In the following Scripture note God's emphasis on unity and oneness. In our Lord's high priestly prayer, just hours before He became the sacrifice for our sin, He prayed:

> "*I will remain in the world no longer, but they are still in the world, and I am coming to you. Holy Father, protect them by the power of your name -- the name you gave me --so that they may be one as we are one. . . . My prayer is not for them alone. I pray also for those who will believe in me through their message, that all of them may be one, Father, just as you are in me and I am in you. May they also be in us so that the world may believe that you have sent me. I have given them the glory that you gave me, that they may be one as we are one."*[278]

Early Christians "*were one in heart and mind. No one claimed that any of his possessions was his own, but they shared everything they had.*"[279] For believers at Rome, Paul prayed: "*May the God who gives endurance and encouragement give you a spirit of unity among yourselves as you follow Christ Jesus, so that with one heart and mouth you may glorify the God and Father of our Lord Jesus Christ. Accept one another, then, just as Christ accepted you, in order to bring praise to God.*"[280] And he exhorted the Ephesian believers, "*Be completely humble*

278 John 17:11, 20-22

279 Acts 4:32

280 Romans 15:5

and gentle; be patient, bearing with one another in love. Make every effort to keep the unity of the Spirit through the bond of peace. There is one body and one Spirit-- just as you were called to one hope when you were called-- one Lord, one faith, one baptism; one God and Father of all, who is over all and through all and in all. . . . Therefore each of you must put off falsehood and speak truthfully to his neighbor, for we are all members of one body."[281] And to the Colossian church he urged, "*Bear with each other and forgive whatever grievances you may have against one another. Forgive as the Lord forgave you. And over all these virtues put on love, which binds them all together in perfect unity. Let the peace of Christ rule in your hearts, since as members of one body you were called to peace. And be thankful.*"[282]

Remember, we saw above that unity is not something we work up from below; God gives it from above. And when Jews and Gentiles become, as it were in Christ a race of many races, the principalities and powers whose great desire is to destroy by dividing and foster discord, are forced to acknowledge God's sovereign wisdom and power.

In the light of these Scriptures, there are two policies that all Christians should practice. 1. If you have a disagreement with anyone, especially your pastor or any other church leader, pray about this, three times a day, for one week before talking to any one else. In most situations, the Lord will take care of the problem. However, if the

---

281 Ephesians 4:2-6; 4:25

282 Colossians 3:13-15

problem still exists, follow the biblical instruction on settling the problem.[283]

2. Satan is *"the accuser of our brethren."*[284] Do not become Satan's coworker by listening to negative comments about people who are not present to defend themselves. Mark this well. Anyone who will speak ill of someone who is not present will also speak ill of you when you are not present.

I urge you to make the following commitment:

> God helping me, I will seek to develop the discipline of praying for the leaders of my church. I will pray for my pastor and his family at each meal, and I will prayer for one other leader and his/her family on a rotating basis each day.

Let me unpack the meaning of these words. Notice I do not ask you to bind your conscience with a vow. The words, "God helping me, I will," means by grace with the aid of the Lord, you will seriously attempt this commitment. The words, "seek to develop the discipline" indicate that a process is involved. It will take time and effort to develop the discipline, but with the effort, in time, this discipline will be a reality for you.

The words, "at each meal" are meant to anchor your prayer for leaders, especially your pastor, to the recurring event of eating. This needs elaboration. Food is not more important for your body than prayer is for your leaders. Each time you eat a meal, pause to thank God for the food and pray

---

[283] See Matthew 18:15-17

[284] Revelation 12:10

for your leaders. This assumes that grace at meals should be a normal part of a Christian's daily life. Some say grace at meals because they developed the habit in childhood. Some say grace before meals served at home but not in public places. Have you ever thought through why Christians give thanks before eating? What is its biblical basis?

Christianity is rooted in Jewish beginnings. To the Jews, prayer is the means by which the people of God stay attuned to the truth that all of life is sacred. The *Talmud*, which contains ancient traditions of the Jews, tells us that a blessing for food was first articulated by Moses in gratitude for the manna that the Israelites ate in the desert.[285] The ancient rabbis taught, "It is forbidden to a man to enjoy anything of this world without a benediction, and if anyone enjoys anything of this world without a benediction, he commits sacrilege."[286] It would be the same as taking something that doesn't belong to us without the permission of the owner. This is so because no aspect of life is devoid of God's presence. "The earth is the Lord's, and everything in it, the world, and all who live in it."[287]

Blessings before and after meals The Jewish sages prescribed blessings to say before eating.[288] It did not matter if one eats a full dinner or a casual snack. The blessings before eating or drinking are part of a broader category of *blessings of enjoyment*, said for things that bring pleasure.

---

[285] Exodus 16:14 ff

[286] *Babylonian Talmud*, Berakhot 35a

[287] Psalms 24:1

[288] See Rabbi Hayim Halevy Donin, *To Pray as a Jew, A Guide to the Prayer Book and the Synagogue Service,* pages 284 ff, 305 ff, Basic Books, 1980.

Moses commanded, "*When you have eaten and are satisfied, praise the LORD your God for the good land he has given you.*"[289] Devout Jews see it as a biblical duty to recite a blessing after eating because when people are sated, they are more likely to forget Him who is the source of their refreshment. It is easier to think of God and be grateful to Him when the food is still before us and we are hungry. It often happens that when people are able comfortably to meet their basic needs, they turn away from God. This is what troubled Moses when he instructed the Israelites. After giving them the command to bless God after eating, Moses expressed his concern:

> *Be careful that you do not forget the LORD your God, failing to observe his commands, his laws and his decrees that I am giving you this day. Otherwise, when you eat and are satisfied, when you build fine houses and settle down, and when your herds and flocks grow large and your silver and gold increase and all you have is multiplied, then your heart will become proud and you will forget the LORD your God, who brought you out of Egypt, out of the land of slavery. He led you through the vast and dreadful desert, that thirsty and waterless land, with its venomous snakes and scorpions. He brought you water out of hard rock. He gave you manna to eat in the desert, something your fathers had never known, to humble and to test you so that in the end it might go well with you. You may say to yourself, "My power and the strength of my hands have produced this wealth for me." But remember the LORD your God, for it is he who gives you the ability to produce wealth, and*

---

289 Deuteronomy 8:10

> *so confirms his covenant, which he swore to your forefathers, as it is today.*[290]

The oldest and most universal of the Jewish blessings is as follows:

> Blessed are You, Lord our God, King of the universe, who in His goodness, grace, loving kindness, and mercy, nourishes the whole world. He gives food to all flesh, for His loving kindness is everlasting. In His great goodness, we have never lacked for food; may we never lack for food, for the sake of His great Name. For He nourishes and sustains all, He does good to all, and prepares food for all His creatures that he created. Blessed art Thou, Lord, who provides food for all.[291]

There is no need to bless the food or drink. Focus your prayer on blessing God, the Creator and Giver. The blessing does not transfer holiness to the object itself, but rather entitles us to properly partake of the world's pleasure. We give thanks to the Lord and thereby acknowledge that the earth is His and we are its caretakers. Jesus followed this custom.[292]

Christ is building His Church to accomplish His work in this world. Doing God's work depends first upon the outpouring of God's love, wisdom and power through continual, fervent prayer. Deeper than the need for great crowds of people, deeper far than the need for money and programs, deep down at the heart and soul of this work, is

---

290 Deuteronomy 8:11-18

291 Marvin R. Wilson, *Our Father Abraham, Jewish Roots of the Christian Faith,* Eerdmans, Grand Rapids, MI, 1989, pp. 157-158.

292 See Matthew 26:26 and Luke 24:30

the need for prevailing prayer. Christ's mission will progress in direct relationship to the focus and fervor of our intercession.

May the Lord remind us at every meal to show our gratitude to Him for His provision of the food that sustains our physical lives. May we also remember, *"man does not live on bread alone but on every word that comes from the mouth of the LORD."*[293] And may this understanding drive us to enter into the struggles of this ministry by interceding for our leaders at every meal. The Prayer Guide found in Appendix Two will help your develop your ability to pray for the leaders and workers of your church.

---

[293] Deuteronomy 8:3; Matthew 4:4; Luke 4:4

Afterword

The Glory of God

We began this book praying with the apostle Paul, "*May He be given glory in the church and in Christ Jesus forever and ever through endless ages. Amen.*"[294]

Glory! Few words have such a diverse array of meanings. The daily paper speaks of new fame or distinctions being awarded an athlete, a musician, or a scientist. On the human level, glory is virtually identical with reputation. It indicates that a person has ample ground for pride and for boasting. In whatever profession, it marks a successful climb to the pinnacle of achievement. Glory, therefore, becomes indispensable in describing the different degrees of success that attends the winners. Therefore, glory is something reserved by society for its heroes and leaders, a term used often to prod individuals to greater effort and to crown those who have fulfilled the expectations.

Observes Minear, "In modern idiom, few things are more vanishing than glory; in the Bible nothing is more eternal. Whereas, in modern idiom few things are less substantial, in the Bible there is usually a stubborn, tough ontological claim. In our ordinary speech we seldom use glory as itself an active and potent reality. We therefore fail to catch the full realism of biblical writers when they speak of God's glory.... *Doxa* (glory) is basically a noun, a substantive. It denotes God's very being: His life, His power, His activity,

---

294 Ephesians 3:21 NLB

His fullness, His grace. God's life is His glory; His glory is His livingness."[295]

God is glorified in the Church and the Church is glorified in God. The New Testament identifies sons as those who inherit God's glory. God glorifies the saints and is glorified in them. To Paul the people of God are those who have received God's glory.[296] To Luke the coming of Christ was the sign that God had begun to fulfill His promise of *"glory of Your people Israel."*[297] Paul calls *"the churches, the glory of Christ."*[298] Jesus prays for the Church, "*And all Mine are Yours, and Yours are Mine, and I am glorified in them.*"[299]

The inspired Apostle exalts, "*But we all, with unveiled face, beholding as in a mirror the glory of the Lord, are being transformed into the same image from glory to glory, just as by the Spirit of the Lord.*"[300] Our lives become enacted doxologies as we learn "*whether you eat or drink, or whatever you do, do all to the glory of God.*"[301] As we in prayer claim God's promises He is glorified. *"For all the promises of God in Him are Yes, and in Him Amen, to the glory of God through us."*[302] For the church to live as the body of Christ means that it embodies *His* glory.[303] We will

---

[295] Minear, *Horizons of Christian Community*, p. 27.

[296] See Romans 9:4

[297] Luke 2:32

[298] 2 Corinthians 8:23

[299] John 17:10

[300] 2 Corinthians 3:18

[301] 1 Corinthians 10:31

[302] 2 Corinthians 1:20

[303] Minear, *Horizons of Christian Community,* p. 34.

never understand the Church apart from understanding this glory. [304]

On completion of seminary, God called me to serve as the pastor-director of the Limestone Larger Parish. Three congregations in rural northern Alabama. In the Nebo community lived Dr. Strong, a Presbyterian pastor then in his late 90s. The first time I called on him I asked how he was and he replied, “I’m one day closer to glory!” Each time I saw him over the next two years he made the same declaration, “I’m one day closer to glory!”

The last time I was with Dr. Strong was unforgettable. He had been taken to the hospital and was not expected to live long. For three days he had been connected to intravenous feeding, he had wasted down to mere skin and bones. He did not have the strength to lift his little finger. I was in his room with members of his family and friends. The nurse attending was a good caregiver, but she was an unbeliever. Suddenly Dr. Strong sat up in bed. His face shone. For almost ten minutes he carried on a conversation with the Lord and his wife -- who had been dead about twenty years. Then he lay back in the bed, the light in his face faded and he entered glory.

Regardless of your age, each day brings you “one day closer to glory.” This is reality! Grasping this truth will move you and your fireteam to cry out, “Thy Kingdom Come!” Then you will pray with kingdom focus for the leaders and workers of your church and it will be invigorated and become all God desires it to be. Then God will regularly add new believers and new congregations to

---

[304] Ibid., 36.

His Church. And you will indeed experience new strength for living to the glory of God!

Discussion Guide

Invigorate Your Church is the sergeant's training manual for stage III of the Kingdom Campaign. To receive full benefit from this manual, you should have already completed the private's training for stage I (***Improve Your Prayer Life***) and the corporal's training for stage II (***Intercede For and With Your Family***). You should now be using the training you received in stage II to help three people in your own fireteam to pray with kingdom focus for and with their family. To properly lead your fireteam, continue to pray 15 minutes (five minutes in the morning for your family, and 10 minutes with your family in the evening, perhaps at mealtime,) using what you learned from ***Intercede For and With Your Family.***[305] Also continue your 15 minutes (10 each morning and 5 each evening) of daily kingdom-focused prayer using what you learned from ***Improve Your Prayer Life.***[306]

The following *Discussion Guide* has been prepared to help you plan how you will work through the material in ***Invigorate Your Church***, as well as how to pray with kingdom focus for the leaders and laborers in your church. I suggest you plan an additional fifteen minutes each day. Before you begin reading the text, be sure to read the introductory material in this *Discussion Guide* (through the *Fireteam Commitment* on page 169), as it will answer many of the questions you may have or will have! It also will

---

305 Ibid., 2000.

306 Ibid.

explain how to use the *Five Appendices*—particularly *Appendices Two*, *Three*, *Four* and *Five*, which are prayer guides.

Each session in the *Discussion Guide* provides instructions for materials to be completed prior to your monthly fireteam meeting.[307] For example, read and work through *Session One* before your team meets the first month. (Fireteams meet once a month, for three months; each meeting lasts two hours. It is assumed that you are familiar with the fireteam concept and that you are studying this book using that format.)

Session instructions include, among other things, study questions to be read prior to reading the material in the text. They also include reading assignments, which will prepare you for discussion in your fireteam meetings. Approximately 60 pages of reading are assigned before each monthly meeting or an average of 2 page per day. (To accomplish this task in five days each week, plan to read on the average of 3 pages each day.) Or perhaps you will want to take an hour once each week to accomplish this task (approx. 15 pages per week). If you decide you want to cover the material in one sitting, do so early in the month so you can reflect on it during your prayer times throughout the month.

Six Learning Activities

Over the next ninety days, it will be best to continue the six activities you learned to use in ***Improve Your Prayer Life***.[308] To refresh your memory, they are:

---

307 See ***The Kingdom Campaign*** booklet, available free from Serve International, for more information on fireteams.

308 Archie Parrish, Serve International, Atlanta, GA, 2000.

- Praying will make you a focused person.
- Reading will make you an informed person.
- Writing will make you an exact person.
- Meeting will make you a bonded person.
- Discussing will make you an insightful person.
- Doing will make you a growing person.

Praying Will Make You a Focused Person

Prayerful study focuses your mind on discovering God's will. At the beginning of each session, you will find the following printed prayer:

> Lord Jesus Christ, You loved the church and gave Yourself for her, to make her holy and clean with the washing of water by the word, that You might present her to Yourself a glorious church, not having spot or wrinkle or any such thing, but that she should be holy and without blemish (Ephes. 5:25-27). Therefore, I pray for my pastor and my church, my teammates and me. Give us helpful insights and understanding from what we study. Show us what we need to understand better. As You show us things we are eager to try, enable us to do them. As You show us things that we find hard to apply to our lives, help us be honest about them. As we review the questions in the *Discussion Guide*, focus our minds and help us find Your truth in what we study. Through this effort, invigorate our local church leaders and workers so that we may better be Your people and faithfully continue Christ's mission.

Start your study right now by meditating on this prayer; make its thoughts yours, and then pray it. Plural pronouns are used so that, in your thinking, you continue to develop a kingdom focus and include others. Write the names of your fireteam members, your family, your pastors and other church leaders, and a few church members and other Christians on the *Prayer List* provided in *Appendix One* on page 185. As you develop your *Prayer List,* don't make it so long that it becomes a burden.

When you study the assigned material, frequently pause and ask the Holy Spirit to give you understanding and discernment. Anytime you find your mind wandering, ask the Lord to refocus your thoughts. As He gives insight, pause and ask Him for grace sufficient to do what He is telling you. Pray for opportunities to share what you learn with others—doing so will cause you to grow in what you are learning.

Reading Will Make You an Informed Person

The writer of the book of Hebrews states, "W*ithout faith it is impossible to please Him, for he who comes to God must believe that He is, and that He is a rewarder of those who diligently seek Him.*"[309] What you receive from reading this book will, to a great degree, be determined by what you expect to receive. Read with expectant faith, and you will receive more of what God desires to give you. Before going any further, pause and complete this sentence in your mind: "From this book I expect to receive ______." Write your expectations on the *Prayer List* provided on page 185. When you finish reading the book, ask yourself if your expectations have been realized.

---

309 Hebrews 11:6

As a member of a fireteam, you agree to read selected material according to a specific schedule. Start each session by rapidly reviewing the material in the *Discussion Guide* for that session. Then read the assigned portions of the book and write in your journal your answers to the *Four Filter Questions* found on page 160, as well as the answers to as many of the discussion questions as time permits.

Three Guards: Your mind will be fast at work as you read. But before you own anything in your heart, it must pass through three guards that protect your heart. Each guard is an automatic reaction. You may be unaware of it, yet you experience it. The three guards are as follows:

The Guard of Understanding: You must understand something to respond properly.

The Ethical Guard: After you understand something, it is more likely that you will do it if you believe it is right. You cannot do what you believe to be wrong without violating your conscience. God's word is *always* right, but some of its teachings may be hard for you to apply. When you find a hard saying, don't just pass over it. Make a note of it. Pray that God will help you properly respond. Share your concern with your fireteam and ask them to pray for you and help you.

The Emotional Guard: If you understand something and believe it is right, but fear that doing it will hurt you more than help you, you will struggle with doing it—or may not even try to do it. At times, you will need to weigh apparent present benefits against actual eternal benefits. Paul put it this way: *"I consider that our present*

> *sufferings are not worth comparing with the glory that will be revealed in us."*[310]

Four Filter Questions: Four questions will help you think through and respond to your three guards. Tuck these in your mind:

1. What helpful insights do I understand from this section? (understanding)
2. What do I want to understand better? (understanding)
3. What is God telling me to do that I'm not afraid to try? (emotional)
4. What is God telling me that I find hard to apply to my life? (ethical or emotional)

You will be reminded to review these *Four Filter Questions* before you begin to read the text. The Bible tells us to search and we will find. Keeping these *Four Filter Questions* in mind will engage your mind to search for truth. At the end of your reading, react to your thoughts in light of these questions by writing your thinking in your journal.

As you read, it may be helpful to do the following:

1. Look for things that you understand and are eager to do. Place an asterisk (*) beside these.
2. Put a question mark (?) beside anything you do not understand.
3. Note anything that threatens you with an "X." Also, indicate why it threatens you.

---

310 Romans 8:18 NIV

Anytime you try to be what the Lord desires, the devil makes sure at some point you feel threatened. Deal with things that frighten you. *"For God has not given us a spirit of fear, but of power and of love and of a sound mind."*[311] If fear is there, face it with a sound mind (self-discipline), pray for spiritual empowerment, and it will vanish.

Writing Will Make You an Exact Person

Life that is worth living is worth recording. It is impossible to overestimate the increased benefit you will gain from each assignment if you will write down your responses to the *Four Filter Questions* and, as time permits, your responses to the questions from the *Discussion Guide*. Obviously, the more you put into this study, the more you will receive from it. When you are in a fireteam, sharing these written thoughts will bless you and others in the team.

All members of the fireteam keep a personal journal. Do not let the thought of writing your answers to the *Four Filter Questions* and the discussion questions in your journal overwhelm you. If you will try investing an average of 15 minutes a day in going through the text, you can easily work through all the material in a month's time.

Here are some practical suggestions for journal keeping:

- Do whatever works for you.
- Make journaling as convenient as possible.
- Carry a notebook for thoughts that occur to you during the day. Some prefer small notebooks they can carry in their coat pocket or purse. Others prefer to use a larger notebook.

---

[311] 2 Timothy 1:7

- If you write your journal in longhand, be sure to write enough to retain your full thought.
- If you are able to use a word processor and one is convenient for you, try it. But, if your access to it is limited, stick to old-fashioned handwriting.
- Don't worry about sentence structure, spelling or penmanship. No one else will see your writing.
- Don't just copy words from the text. Express your thoughts in your own words.
- Throughout the *Discussion Guide*, you will see questions such as, "Do you agree? Why?" It is important to think these questions through. Don't blindly accept the thoughts in the text.

Now, before going any further, stop, take your journal, and copy from your *Prayer List* (on page 185) your answer to this statement: "From this book I expect to receive ______________________________________."

The *Fireteam Commitment* form on page 169 is for you to sign (if you have not already done so) as a reminder of your responsibilities to God and to the other members of your fireteam. Copy your *Fireteam Commitment* into your journal. Why? Before a man was crowned king over Israel, he was required to write the law of the covenant in his own hand. This reinforced his knowledge of his responsibilities under this covenant. This handwritten copy of the law was evidence that he willingly assumed the covenant's responsibilities.[312]

---

312 *"When he takes the throne of his kingdom, he is to write for himself on a scroll a copy of this law, taken from that of the priests, who are Levites. It is to be with him, and he is to read it all the days of his life so that he may learn to revere the LORD his God and follow carefully all the words of this law and these decrees."* Deuteronomy 17:18-19 NIV

Make journal-keeping a life-long habit, and you will find new depth in your relationship with Jesus.

Meeting Will Make You a Bonded Person

If you are not involved in a fireteam, consider joining one. Doing so will provide encouragement, understanding and accountability to you, as well as to others in the group. Remember that you will receive most from this effort if you regularly discuss this material with other believers. This may be challenging, but it should not be overwhelming.

Fireteams meet for three two-hour monthly meetings at an agreed upon time and place. The meeting place should be free from unnecessary distractions. It should be a place where you can easily talk to each other and pray.

Fireteam members pray for each other daily. If one is absent from the team meeting, the leader should make contact to see that the team member stays current on the matters of the fireteam. As members grow closer to one another, they will ask to be encouraged for more and more significant matters in their lives. Becoming a kingdom intercessor is serious business! The devil will attack the members of the fireteam in a variety of ways—you need each other's support.

Discussing Will Make You an Insightful Person

In the fireteam meeting, the members discuss their written responses. The discussion should take about one hour of your two-hour meeting. You will probably not have time to discuss all the questions provided in the *Discussion Guide* for each session. Your fireteam leader will deal with specific questions, but **most of the discussion time will be**

focused on responses to the *Four Filter Questions*. Be prepared to express your thinking in these small groups by reviewing your journal prior to the meeting, and, if necessary, consolidating your thoughts or choosing the three most significant issues you want to discuss. Important insights gained from the discussion should be noted in your journal.

Doing Will Make You a Growing Person

The Apostle James exhorts:

> *Do not merely listen to the word, and so deceive yourselves. Do what it says. Anyone who listens to the word but does not do what it says is like a man who looks at his face in a mirror and, after looking at himself, goes away and immediately forgets what he looks like. But the man who looks intently into the perfect law that gives freedom, and continues to do this, not forgetting what he has heard, but doing it—he will be blessed in what he does.*[313]

It is an old saying that, "Knowledge is power." The words of James make it clear that knowledge without proper action is NOT power; rather it brings judgment! Maturity can always be determined by how long it takes us to do what we know is the will of God. The more mature Christian obeys more quickly, the less mature Christian takes longer.

Obedience is the supreme test of faith in God and reverence for Him. *"Samuel replied: 'Does the LORD delight in burnt offerings and sacrifices as much as in obeying the voice of the LORD? To obey is better than sacrifice, and to heed is*

---

313 James 1:22-25

better than the fat of rams.'"[314] No one can sustain a right relationship with the Lord without obedience. Every thought must be made captive to and obedient to Christ.[315] Nothing less than "wholehearted" obedience to the truth is acceptable to God.[316] Therefore, each team member seeks to do what he or she believes the Lord is directing. Specific action-steps should be shared with the group. Before the close of each meeting, time should be spent praying for one another. At the beginning of each session, there should be a brief time of reporting on progress in these actions.

In summary, insight will come to those who pray and read. Greater understanding will come to those who, in addition to prayer and reading, record their responses to the *Four Filter Questions* and the exercises in the *Discussion Guide* in a personal journal and then regularly meet to discuss this with other Christians. But, ultimate benefit will come only to those who add obedience to all these steps and do God's will as He reveals it through this process.

The Discipline of Praying

In addition to studying the material in this book, it is important that you develop the ability to pray with kingdom focus for the leaders and workers of your local church so that it becomes all that God desires—being His people and faithfully continuing Christ's mission. In order to develop this as a discipline, plan to add five minutes to your prayer time at each meal. This additional 15 minutes of prayer

---

[314] 1 Samuel 15:22 NIV

[315] See 2 Corinthians 10:5

[316] See Romans 6:17 NIV

would be added to the 15 minutes of prayer developed in ***Improve Your Prayer Life,***[317] and the second 15 minutes developed in ***Intercede For and With Your Family.***[318] The daily total would now be 45 minutes—15 minutes in the morning, 5 minutes at breakfast, 5 at lunch, 15 at dinner, and 5 in the evening.) Of course, the times mentioned here are approximate. Don't set a timer and stop when it indicates you have "put in" the appropriate time. When the Lord blesses you with His presence, rejoice in Him and forget the time. The Suggested Daily Time Investment chart on page 168 shows you how the stages of the Kingdom Campaign training help you build the discipline of daily kingdom-focused prayer.

Spend the additional five minutes you are adding at each meal as follows:

1. Read aloud the assigned prayer guide material
2. Think: What does this mean? How can it become my prayer?
3. Pray aloud for your church leaders and workers.

Praying aloud helps you keep your mind and heart focused. Praying the selected Scripture for the leaders and workers of your local church will facilitate the Holy Spirit's work in their hearts and increase their ability to lead the whole church to be the people of God and faithfully continue Christ's mission. Therefore, this stage of your fireteam training is very important.

The material in the prayer guides in *Appendices Two and Three* will take a total of ninety days to complete. Each day

---

[317] Archie Parrish, Serve International, Atlanta, GA, 2000.

[318] Ibid.

ask the Lord to enable you to pray the next day. However, if you miss a day during the week, don't be discouraged. You might be able to have more extended time later in the week.

Again, I encourage you—and challenge you—to make the next ninety days a period of extraordinary kingdom-focused prayer for your local church. Jesus promised, "*On this rock I will build My church, and the gates of Hades shall not prevail against it.*"[319] "*If you abide in Me, and My words abide in you, you will ask what you desire, and it shall be done for you.*"[320] As we in prayer claim God's promises He is glorified. "*For all the promises of God in Him are Yes, and in Him Amen, to the glory of God through us.*"[321] May we claim Christ's promises until He defeats hell and completes His Church.

•••••

---

319 Matthew 16:18

320 John 15:7

321 2 Corinthians 1:20

Suggested Daily Time Investment

(In minutes)

	Stage		
	I	II	III
Early Morning	**10**	10+**5**	10+5
Breakfast			**5**
Lunch			**5**
Dinner		**10**	10+**5**
Evening	**5**	5	5
Total	15	30	45

Stage I: You begin to improve your prayer life using a daily prayer guide[322] to develop the discipline of praying 15 minutes a day, 10 in the morning and 5 in the evening.

Stage II: You intercede for and with your family, adding 15 minutes of daily prayer time, 5 in the morning interceding for your family and 10 at dinner interceding with your family using the *Daily Prayer Guide.*[323]

Stage III: You seek to invigorate your church, adding another 15 minutes of daily prayer for its leaders and laborers—5 minutes at each meal using Prayer Guides.

---

[322] Found in ***Improve Your Prayer Life.***

[323] Found in ***Intercede For and With Your Family***, Archie Parrish, Serve International, Atlanta, GA, 2000.

Fireteam Commitment

I desire that the Holy Spirit invigorate my local church. To this end, I covenant with the Lord and members of my fireteam to meet ______ times:

____

____

____

(Insert scheduled dates and times)

God helping me, I will seek to add 15 minutes to my daily prayer and invest this time praying for the leaders and workers of my local church. I will read the selected material as scheduled. I will write my responses to the four filter questions and as many of the discussion questions as time allows. I will meet with the other members of my team at

____

(Insert location)

____

Signature Date

Session One

Before you begin to prepare for this session, pray:

> Lord Jesus Christ, You loved the church and gave Yourself for her, to make her holy and clean with the washing of water by the word, that You might present her to Yourself a glorious church, not having spot or wrinkle or any such thing, but that she should be holy and without blemish (Ephes. 5:25-27).
> Therefore, I pray for my pastor and my local church, my teammates and me. Give us helpful insights and understanding from what we study. Show us what we need to understand better. As You show us things we are eager to try, enable us to do them. As You show us things that we find hard to apply to our lives, help us be honest about them. As we review the questions in the *Discussion Guide*, focus our minds and help us find Your truth in what we study. Through this effort, invigorate our local church leaders and workers so that we may better be Your people and faithfully continue Christ's mission.

I. If you have not read the booklet, ***The Kingdom Campaign***,[324] please do so before your next fireteam meeting. This booklet explains why this ministry is necessary and how to implement it.

---

[324] Available free from Serve International.

II. Read *Before You Begin* starting on page 13 and the introductory remarks of this *Discussion Guide* (pages 155 through 156). As necessary, review the Six Learning Activities found on page 156 and use them as you prepare for *Session One* with your fireteam. Review the questions below for each section before you read it. This will put your mind in "search mode" and enable you to get more from your reading.

III. Read *the introduction to Appendix Two* (page 189) *of the General Prayer Guide.* Begin praying daily at each meal for the leaders of your church.

IV. Write the following Scriptures on a card; carry it with you and read it aloud frequently. You will be asked to recite or read this verse in your fireteam meeting.

Now to Him who is able to do exceedingly abundantly above all that we ask or think, according to the power that works in us, to Him be glory in the church by Christ Jesus to all generations, forever and ever. Amen. (Ephesians 3:14-21).

He who has clean hands shall grow stronger and stronger (Job 17:9).

V. Review the Four Filter Questions found on page 160. Read *The Church Deceived* and *What Is The Church* (pages 19 through 72) and write in your journal the answers to the Four Filter Questions.

VI. Answer as many of the following questions as time allows.

1. To a great degree, the American Church in its passion for worldly success has departed from *"the*

simplicity that is in Christ." Consequently, it does not function as a militant army engaged in spiritual combat, rather it is more like a corporation engaged in competitive peacetime business. (See p. 20). Do you agree with this? Why?

2. Does your church act as a "peacetime business" or a "wartime army"? (page 20). Explain why you answered as you did.

What is the Church?

3. "One thing more contrary to Christianity than all heresies and all schisms combined is to play Christianity, like the child plays soldier, taking away the danger and in its place to introduce power, worldly goods, advantages, and luxurious enjoyment" (p. 41). Do you agree with this? Why?

4. How do most Christians determine in which local church they are supposed to be a member? (p . 46)

5. The first of General Sun Tzu's five fundamental factors for war is moral influence. What did he mean by this and how does it apply to leadership in the church? (p. 48)

6. The church is a charismatic community, which means God gives *every believer* spiritual gifts and expects these gifts to be used to enable the church to be His people and faithfully continue Christ's mission (p. 50). Do you agree with this? Why?

7. The early Church had a holy rhythm of nurture and mission. It gathered on the Lord's Day for nurture —worship, teaching and fellowship--ministry to the

body. And then it scattered throughout the week for mission—work, mercy, service, and witness -- ministry in and to the world. (p. 58). How much of this "holy rhythm" is present in your church.

8. What is the difference between witness and evangelism? (p. 59)
9. "In the eyes of God, all is sacred and nothing is secular". Do you agree with this? Why or why not? (p. 60)
10. "...one of the most significant factors causing (pastoral) burnout is the lack of (their) actually having one in seven for their **own** personal day of worship and rest." (p. 61). Does your church insure that your pastor regularly has a day off each week?
11. "Working with ...eternal perspective will make whatever we do spiritual ministry". (p. 61) Do you agree or disagree? Why or why not?
12. "From God's perspective, death is never untimely, and it is never final" (p. 67) What does this quote mean to you?
13. Examine yourself as described on pages 71-72. This assignment will take about one hour to complete so, you might wish to break it up into multiple shorter periods. Follow the step-by-step directions. The people to whom you need to make confession and restitution should be added to your prayer list.

•••••

Session Two

Before you begin to prepare for this session, pray:

> Lord Jesus Christ, You loved the church and gave Yourself for her, to make her holy and clean with the washing of water by the word, that You might present her to Yourself a glorious church, not having spot or wrinkle or any such thing, but that she should be holy and without blemish (Ephes. 5:25-27). Therefore, I pray for my pastor and my church, my teammates and me. Give us helpful insights and understanding from what we study. Show us what we need to understand better. As You show us things we are eager to try, enable us to do them. As You show us things that we find hard to apply to our lives, help us be honest about them. As we review the questions in the *Discussion Guide*, focus our minds and help us find Your truth in what we study. Through this effort, invigorate our local church leaders and workers so that we may better be Your people and faithfully continue Christ's mission.

I. Review the Six Learning Activities found beginning on page 156 and use them as you prepare for *Session Two* with your fireteam. Review the questions below for each section before you read it. This will put your mind in search mode and enable you to get more from your reading.

II. Continue praying daily at each meal for the leaders of your church, using the Prayer Guide in *Appendix Two.*

III. Write the following scriptures on a card; carry it with you and read it aloud frequently. You will be asked to recite or read this verse in your fireteam meeting.

Search me, O God, and know my heart; try me, and know my anxieties; and see if there is any wicked way in me, and lead me in the way everlasting" (Psalm 139:23, 24).

But we all, with unveiled face, beholding as in a mirror the glory of the Lord, are being transformed into the same image from glory to glory, just as by the Spirit of the Lord (2 Corinthians 3:18).

V. Review the Four Filter Questions found on page 160. Read *What is Vigor?* and *How Does a Church Regain Vigor?* (p. 73-122) and write in your journal the answers to the Four Filter Questions.

VI. Answer as many of the following questions as time allows.

What is Vigor?

1. "Continual vigilance is essential to avoid the loss of vigor." (p. 76) Do you agree with this? Why?

2. "Individual physical aging and organizational aging is inevitable and properly dealing with the changes produced by aging can increase church vigor." (p. 90). Is your church experiencing an "aging challenge"? If so, how is your churches leadership dealing with it?

3. “There is no success in ministry without successors.” (pg. 95) Do you agree with this? Why? Does your church’s leadership have a strategy to develop future leaders for the church?

4. “It is not enough to renew individual hearts for churches to be renewed, although it is probably true that structural renewal cannot progress very far unless it is preceded by a great deal of individual awakening.” (p. 96) Do you agree with this? Why or why not?

5. “A sin of omission means not doing what Scripture says we should do. For example, any person who is not using his or her spiritual gifts is sinning.” (p. 79) Do you agree with this? Why or why not?

How Does a Church Regain Vigor?

6. “Of course it is true that faith begins in stillness of heart, and it must constantly be returning to quiet communion with God, but when it remains only on the inside, it decomposes, and becomes a musty, unventilated piety. On the other hand, when it seeks only the outside it withers and becomes sterile in a Christian busyness that is cut off from the eternal springs.” (p. 99) Describe the balance that seems necessary for a vital personal faith.

7. “Only by a conscious and continuing nurture of his inner life can any man avoid the tragedy of killing the thing he loves. The man who supposes that he has not time to pray or to reflect, because the social tasks are so numerous and urgent, will soon find that he has become fundamentally unproductive, because he has

separated his life from its roots." (p. 99) How has your schedule of time alone with the LORD gone lately? How can this time be protected and insured?

8. "One who is genuinely repentant will perform three acts (confess, repay and watch) that demonstrate the reality of his penitence." (p. 105) Write down a specific sin that you have committed recently, as well as how you could possibly repay, and how and when you will do so. Now pray about this matter again …and watch.

9. "Loving, firm, and consistent discipline is essential for the unity, purity, holiness, and apostolicity of each local church." (p. 106) How effective is your church's discipline ministry? How could it be more biblical? Pray for your church's leadership as they perform this often difficult ministry.

10. "Works of restitution do not save, but they demonstrate that repentance is genuine" (p. 108) "Making restitution can provide fruitful opportunity for witness" (p. 108). Do you agree with these statements? Why or why not?

•••••

Session Three

Before you begin to prepare for this session, pray:

> Lord Jesus Christ, You loved the church and gave Yourself for her, to make her holy and clean with the washing of water by the word, that You might present her to Yourself a glorious church, not having spot or wrinkle or any such thing, but that she should be holy and without blemish (Ephes. 5:25-27). Therefore, I pray for my pastor and my church, my teammates and me. Give us helpful insights and understanding from what we study. Show us what we need to understand better. As You show us things we are eager to try, enable us to do them. As You show us things that we find hard to apply to our lives, help us be honest about them. As we review the questions in the *Discussion Guide*, focus our minds and help us find Your truth in what we study. Through this effort, invigorate our local church leaders and workers so that we may better be Your people and faithfully continue Christ's mission.

I. Review the Six Learning Activities found beginning on page 156 and use them as you prepare for *Session Three* with your fireteam. Review the questions below for each section before you read it. This will put your mind in search mode and enable you to get more from your reading.

II. Continue praying daily at each meal for the leaders of your church using the Prayer Guide in *Appendix Two.*

III. Write the following Scriptures on a card; carry it with you and read it *aloud* frequently. You will be asked to recite or read this verse in your fireteam meeting.

If you abide in me and my words abide in your, you shall ask what you will and it shall be done. (John 15:7)

Pray without ceasing. 1 Thessalonians 5:17

IV. Review the Four Filter Questions found on page 160. Read *How Does a Church Maintain Vigor?* and *Armorbearer Intercessors Ministry* and *Afterword* (p. 123-154*), and Appendix Five: How to Pray for Missionaries* (p. 245) and *Chaplains* (p. 256), and write in your journal the answers to the Four Filter Questions.

V. Answer as many of the following questions as time allows.

How Does a Church Maintain Vigor?

1. What are the two God-ordained channels of His grace to human souls? (p. 125). Do you personally see prayer as being as potentially powerful in your spiritual life as the scriptures are? Why do you think this is true?

2. "..prayer is a usual and necessary means for all gracious growth". (p. 126) How does Robert Dabney support this position? How might this explain an individual or church's lack of spiritual growth?

Armorbearer Intercessors Ministry

3. What are two goals of the Armorbearer Intercessor's Ministry? (p. 128).

4. Wherever he can, Satan seeks to deceive, disgrace and *then* destroy. (p. 132) Do you agree or disagree with this statement? Why or why not? How might this knowledge impact your personal prayers?

5. "Self-reliance needed to be sifted from the Twelve before God could use them to the full." (p. 133) How can self-reliance be an obstruction to spiritual growth?

6. "If you have a disagreement with anyone, especially your pastor or any other church leader, pray about this, three times a day, for one week before talking to any one else. If the problem still exists, follow the biblical instruction (Matthew 18:15-17) for reconciling the matter." (p. 145) How might your church be different if all its members followed this policy?

7. "Satan is 'the accuser of our brethren.' Do not become Satan's coworker by listening to negative comments about people who are not present to defend themselves. Mark this well, anyone who will speak ill of someone who is not present will also speak ill of you when you are not present." (p. 146) Is this an issue in your life? If so, how? Repent and go ask forgiveness from those involved.

8. We often refer to prayers at mealtime as "giving the blessing". If you use this term, what is your

understanding the word "blessing" in this sentence? (p. 149) What are some reasons to pray at mealtime?

9. Paul Minear wrote: "In modern idiom, few things are more vanishing than glory; in the Bible nothing is more eternal". (p. 151) How does worldly glory differ from Godly glory?

How to Pray for Missionaries and Chaplains

10. Pick a missionary that you or your church supports financially. Write out a prayer for your selected missionary, incorporating the 12 targets suggested by Ron Shaw in Appendix Five.

11. Pick a chaplain that you or your church supports financially. Using the guide in Appendix Five, (p. 245) write out a prayer for that chaplain, incorporating the 11 targets identified by David Peterson.

•••••

Appendices

Appendix One

My Prayer List

From this book, I expect to receive

____

____

____

Obtain from your church office a directory or a list of members and regular guests from your local church. This directory should have a list of all the official leaders and ministry team members. It should also have a list of the workers needed to extend Christ's mission into the neighborhood surrounding the church building. Copies are usually available.

Write in the blanks below the names of individuals for whom you will pray for the next ninety days. When you finish the list, note how many are from a racial, social or economic group other than your own. If there are none, ask God what He desires you to do about this.

To your list of local church leaders I suggest that you add specific missionaries and chaplains. These two groups are on the leading edge of spiritual combat with the world, the flesh and the devil.

Fireteam Members

1.____

2.____

3.____

Family Members

1.____

2.____

3.____

4.____

Pastors

1.____

2.____

Church Leaders

1.____

2.____

3.____

4.____

5.____

6.____

Missionaries

1.______________________________________

2.______________________________________

3.______________________________________

Chaplain

1.______________________________________

Church Members

1.______________________________________

2.______________________________________

3.______________________________________

4.______________________________________

5.______________________________________

6.______________________________________

Church Workers

Current:

1.______________________________________

2.______________________________________

3.______________________________________

4.______________________________________

Needed:

1.____

2.____

3.____

Appendix Two

Prayer Guide

The following prayer guide should be used three times daily for the next sixty days. It suggests a three-step process for kingdom-focused prayer for the leaders and workers of your church. First, read a specific scripture passage. Second, think about the meaning of the passage. You will find it helpful to jot this thinking in your journal. Third, turn your understanding of the scripture into "echo prayer." Each time you pray, pray for yourself and your family. In this stage of training we also urge you to pray by name for leaders and workers of your church. Especially remember your pastor and his family at each meal every day. Also, each day select one other lay leader (elder, deacon, staff, teacher, etc.) and pray by name for that person and his or her family at each meal. Use the daily suggestions from the prayer guide for both your individual prayer time and your family worship.

Begin your prayer time at breakfast by reading aloud the scripture for the day. Then think about what this scripture means and what are its implications for you and those for whom you are praying. Jot these thoughts in your journal and then turn these thoughts into prayer. At lunch and dinner, use the prayer that you developed in the morning. Days 1-7 provide sample prayer built on the scripture selection for each day. In these sample prayers you will see the following words in bold type: **my pastor, the leaders of my church, our missionaries and chaplains.** Where you see this, insert the names of specific people and their families. These sample prayers are not provided for

Days 8 through 56. Ask the Holy Spirit to guide you in writing your own for those days. Day 57–60 focus on praying Psalms 1 and 23. Sample prayers are provided for Psalm 1, ask the Holy Spirit to guide you in praying Psalm 23. Each time you pray, you should "Add other specific requests," that is timely needs of which you are aware.

Daily Prayer

Day 1

Read: *"Return, O backsliding children," says the Lord; "for I am married to you. I will take you, one from a city and two from a family, and I will bring you to Zion. And I will give you shepherds according to My heart, who will feed you with knowledge and understanding. ...I will set up shepherds over them who will feed them; and they shall fear no more, nor be dismayed, nor shall they be lacking," says the Lord. (Jeremiah 3:14-15; 23:4)*

Think:

Pray**:** Father, the great mystery of Your marriage to Your people is beyond my full understanding. Pour out Your grace on the shepherds you have given our local church. Make **my pastor, the leaders of my church, our missionaries and chaplains** shepherds according to Your heart, who will feed us with knowledge and understanding so that we shall fear no more, nor be dismayed, nor shall we be lacking. (Add other specific requests).

Day 2

Read: *The elders who are among you I exhort, I who am a fellow elder and a witness of the sufferings of Christ, and also a partaker of the glory that will be revealed: Shepherd the flock of God which is among you, serving as overseers, not by compulsion but willingly, not for* *dishonest gain but eagerly; nor as being lords over those entrusted to you, but being examples to the flock; and when the Chief Shepherd appears, you will receive the crown of glory that does not fade away.* (1 Peter 5:1-4)

Think:

Pray: Father, enable the elders You have given us, **my pastor, the leaders of my church, our missionaries and chaplains,** to properly shepherd this flock of God, serving as overseers, not by compulsion but willingly, not for dishonest gain but eagerly; nor as being lords over those entrusted to them, but being examples to the flock. Inspire them with the reality that when the Chief Shepherd appears, they will receive the crown of glory that does not fade away. (1 Peter 5:1-4)

(Add other specific requests.)

Day 3

Read: *Hear my cry, O God; attend to my prayer. From the end of the earth I will cry to You, when my heart is overwhelmed; lead me to the rock that is higher than I. For You have been a shelter for me, a strong tower from the enemy.* (Psalm 61:1-3) *I discipline my body and bring it into subjection, lest, when I have preached to others, I myself should become disqualified.* (1 Corinthians 9:27).

Think:

Pray: Father, enable **my pastor, the leaders of my church, our missionaries and chaplains** to acknowledge by prayer their dependency on You for spiritual strength and victory. May they cry to You for help. Show them the importance of fellowship. May they draw great strength and encouragement from those around them who are engaged in the same struggles. May there never be a blight of any kind of sin that taints their reputations or puts their character in question. (Add other specific requests.)

Day 4

Read: *The Lord said, "Simon, Simon! Indeed, Satan has asked for you, that he may sift you as wheat. But I have prayed for you, that your faith should not fail; and when you have returned to Me, strengthen your brethren." But he said to Him, "Lord, I am ready to go with You, both to prison and to death." Then He said, "I tell you, Peter, the rooster shall not crow this day before you will deny three times that you know Me.* (Lk. 22: 31-34)

Think:

***Pray*:** Father, as Satan asked to sift the leaders of the early church, now he seeks to sift **my pastor, the leaders of my church, our missionaries and chaplains.**. Lord Jesus, You prayed for Peter that his faith would not fail and that he would strengthen his brothers. Keep my pastor and the other leaders of my church from the sin of self-confidence. Keep them from falling into sin that disqualifies them from ministry. Do not let Satan undermine their integrity as spiritual leaders, destroying their ministry and bringing reproach upon Christ. Enable them to guard their thoughts and actions carefully. (Add other specific requests.)

Day 5

Read: *Now may the God of patience and comfort grant you to be like-minded toward one another, according to Christ Jesus, that you may with one mind and one mouth glorify the God and Father of our Lord Jesus Christ.* (Romans 15:5-6 NIV)

Think:

Pray: Father, give **my pastor, the leaders of my church, our missionaries and chaplains** endurance and encouragement, allow them to live in harmony with each other by following the example of Christ Jesus. Enable them to have the same goal and praise You, the God and

Father of our Lord Jesus Christ. (Add other specific requests.)

Day 6

***Read**: "And I will pour on the house of David and on the inhabitants of Jerusalem the Spirit of grace and supplication; then they will look on Me whom they pierced. Yes, they will mourn for Him as one mourns for his only son, and grieve for Him as one grieves for a firstborn."* (Zech. 12:10)

Think:

***Pray*:** Father, pour out Your Spirit of grace and supplication on our congregation. Enable us to pray earnestly for the strength of **my pastor, the leaders of my church, our missionaries and chaplains.** Because they are visible leaders, the devil attacks them with more severe temptations than most Christians will ever experience. And You sometimes allow this so that sin can be sifted from their lives and they can better lead the forces of truth and light against the kingdom of darkness. Make my pastor, the leaders of my church and their families holy. Keep them from becoming like stained glass windows—mere religious symbols that alters the pure light of God. (Add other specific requests.)

Day 7

***Read**: "Your word I have hidden in my heart, that I might not sin against You . . . You are already clean because of the word which I have spoken to you."* (Psalm 119:11; John 15:3)

Think:

Pray: Father, protect **my pastor, the leaders of my church, our missionaries and chaplains** from the onslaughts of Satan by proper use of Scripture, prayer, and fellowship. They are already clean because of the word that You have spoken to them. Help them to daily hide Your Word in their hearts that they might not sin against You. Never let them grow complacent in their commitment to You and Your Word. Add other specific requests. (Add other specific requests.)

Day 8

Praying for Virtuous Leadership

The next fifteen days of this guide contain brief explanations of fifteen virtues Paul says are necessary for official leaders of local congregations. Select one virtue daily, read the material on that virtue at each mealtime that day, then pray by name for the people on your prayer list.

Read: *This is a faithful saying: If a man desires the position of a bishop, he desires a good work. A bishop then must be* ***blameless…*** (1 Timothy 3:1-2) Blameless does not mean sinless; it means that at present no legitimate legal or moral charge can be brought against the person. Spiritual leaders must be blameless because they set the example for the congregation to follow. That is a high standard, but it isn't a double standard, since you are responsible to follow the example of your godly leaders (Heb. 13:7, 17), God requires blamelessness of you as well. The difference is that certain sins can disqualify church leaders for life, whereas that's not necessarily true for less prominent roles in the church. Nevertheless, God requires blameless-ness of all believers.[325]

Think:

Pray: (Add other specific requests.)

---

[325] Many of the following definitions are drawn from John McArthur's *The Master's Plan for the Church,* Moody Press, Chicago, IL, 1991.

Day 9

Read: *This is a faithful saying: If a man desires the position of a bishop, he desires a good work. A bishop then must be* ***... the husband of one wife ...***(1 Timothy 3:1-2)

This phrase is more accurately translated "**one-woman man." It doesn't refer to marital status at all** Paul is giving moral qualifications for spiritual leadership, not outlining what an elder's social status or external condition is to be. "One-woman man" speaks of the man's character, the state of his heart. If he is married, he is to be devoted solely to his wife. Whether or not he is married, he is not to be a ladies' man.

Think:

Pray: (Add other specific requests.)

Day 10

Read: *This is a faithful saying: If a man desires the position of a bishop, he desires a good work. A bishop then must be* ***... temperate ...***(1 Timothy 3:1-2)

"A **temperate** person lives deeply. His pleasures are not primarily those of the senses, like the pleasures of a drunkard for instance, but those of the soul. He is filled with spiritual and moral earnestness. He is not given to excess (in the use of wine, etc.), but is moderate, well-balanced, calm, careful, steady, and sane. This pertains to his physical, moral, and mental tastes and habits"[326]

Drinking is only one area in which excess can occur. Overeating has been called the preacher's sin, and often that's a just criticism. But spiritual leaders are to be moderate and balanced in every area of life.

Think:

Pray: (Add other specific requests.)

---

326 William Hendriksen, *Exposition of the Pastoral Epistles,* Grand Rapids: Baker, 1981, p. 122.

Day 11

Read: *This is a faithful saying: If a man desires the position of a bishop, he desires a good work. A bishop then must be* ***… sober-minded…*** (1 Timothy 3:1-2)

The Greek word translated "sober-minded" speaks of discipline or self-control. It's the result of being temperate. The temperate man avoids excess so that he can see things clearly, and that clarity of thought leads to an orderly, disciplined life. He knows how to order his priorities. A sober-minded person is serious about spiritual things. Such a man doesn't have the reputation of a clown. That doesn't mean he avoids humor—any good leader is able to use and enjoy humor. But he is to have an appreciation for what really matters in life.

"Whatever things are true, whatever things are noble, whatever things are just, whatever things are pure, whatever things are lovely, whatever things are of good report, if there is any virtue and if there is anything praiseworthy--meditate on these things" (Phil. 4:8). This is the focus of an ordered and well-disciplined mind.

Think:

Pray: (Add other specific requests.)

Day 12

Read: *This is a faithful saying: If a man desires the position of a bishop, he desires a good work. A bishop then must be* ***… of good behavior …***(1 Timothy 3:1-2)

A man of "good behavior" approaches all the aspects of his life in a systematic, orderly manner. This kind of person diligently fulfills his many duties and responsibilities. His disciplined mind produces disciplined actions— "good behavior." Elders must not have a chaotic lifestyle. That's because their work involves administration, oversight, scheduling, and establishing priorities.

Think:

Pray: (Add other specific requests.)

Day 13

Read: *This is a faithful saying: If a man desires the position of a bishop, he desires a good work. A bishop then must be* ***… hospitable …***(1 Timothy 3:1-2)

Biblical hospitality is showing kindness to strangers, not friends. Jesus said, "When you give a luncheon or a dinner, do not invite your friends or your brothers or your relatives or rich neighbors, lest they also invite you in return, and repayment come to you. But when you give a reception, invite the poor, the crippled, the lame, the blind, and you will be blessed, since they do not have the means to repay you; for you will be repaid at the resurrection of the righteous." (Luke 14:12-14 NASB)

Showing love toward strangers requires vulnerability and can even be dangerous because some may take advantage of your kindness. Whereas God doesn't ask us to discard wisdom and discernment as we deal with strangers (cf. Matt. 10:16), He does require us to love them by being hospitable (Rom. 12:13; Heb. 13:2; 1 Pet. 4:9).

Think:

Pray: (Add other specific requests.)

Day 14

Read: *This is a faithful saying: If a man desires the position of a bishop, he desires a good work. A bishop then must be* ***… able to teach…*** (1 Timothy 3:1-2)

Able to teach is the only qualification listed here that relates to the *function* of an elder and sets the elder apart from the deacon. Elders must be skilled in teaching. They must have the ability to communicate God's Word and the integrity to make their teaching believable. The most powerful impetus to effective teaching is credibility. A skilled teacher will practice what he preaches.

Think:

Pray: (Add other specific requests.)

Day 15

Read: *This is a faithful saying: If a man desires the position of a bishop, he desires a good work. A bishop then must be **... not given to wine...*** (1 Timothy 3:1, 3)

Given to wine means "one who drinks." It doesn't refer to a drunkard—that's an obvious disqualification. The issue here is the man's reputation: Is he notorious for his drinking?

Think:

Pray: (Add other specific requests.)

Day 16

Read: *This is a faithful saying: If a man desires the position of a bishop, he desires a good work. [2] A bishop then must be **... not violent ...***(1 Timothy 3:1, 3)

Elders do not settle disputes with their fists or in other violent ways. An elder isn't quick-tempered and doesn't resort to unnecessary physical violence. This qualification is closely related to 'not given to wine" because such violence is usually connected with people who drink excessively. A spiritual leader must be able to handle things with a cool mind and a gentle spirit.

Think:

Pray: (Add other specific requests.)

Day 17

Read: *This is a faithful saying: If a man desires the position of a bishop, he desires a good work. A bishop then must be **... gentle ...***(1 Timothy 3:1, 3)[327]

The gentle person is considerate, genial, forbearing, or gracious. In a practical sense, the gentle person is able to remember good and forget evil. He doesn't keep a record

---

[327] We skipped "not greedy for money," which appears in the King James Version and the New King James Version but not in the many Greek manuscripts. That qualification is identical in meaning to "not covetous" (v. 3), which we will soon cover.

of wrongs people have committed against him. (See 1 Cor. 13:5)

Think:

Pray: (Add other specific requests.)

Day 18

Read: *This is a faithful saying: If a man desires the position of a bishop, he desires a good work. A bishop then must be* ***… not quarrelsome…*** (1 Timothy 3:1, 3)

When you have a plurality of church leaders attempting to make decisions, you can't get very far if any of them are quarrelsome. That's why Paul said, "The servant of the Lord must not strive, but be gentle unto all men . . . patient". (2 Tim. 2:24) He must be a peacemaker.

Think:

Pray: (Add other specific requests.)

Day 19

Read: *This is a faithful saying: If a man desires the position of a bishop, he desires a good work. A bishop then must be* ***… not covetous…*** (1 Timothy 3:1, 3)

Not covetous speaks of someone who doesn't love money. Love of money can corrupt a man's ministry because it tempts him to view people as a means by which he can get more money. Paul said, *"Now godliness with contentment is great gain. For we brought nothing into this world, and it is certain we can carry nothing out. And having food and clothing, with these we shall be content. But those who desire to be rich fall into temptation and a snare, and into many foolish and harmful lusts which drown men in destruction and perdition. For the love of money is a root of all kinds of evil, for which some have strayed from the faith in their greediness, and pierced themselves through with many sorrows."* (1 Tim. 6:6-10)

Think:

Pray: (Add other specific requests.)

Day 20

Read: *This is a faithful saying: If a man desires the position of a bishop, he desires a good work. A bishop then must be* ***... one who rules his own house well, having his children in submission with all reverence [for if a man does not know how to rule his own house, how will he take care of the church of God?]*** (1 Timothy 3:1, 4-5).

Before an elder can lead in the church he must demonstrate his spiritual leadership within the context of his family. He must be a strong spiritual leader in the home before he is qualified to lead in the church. By implication a man's home includes his resources. A man may love the Lord and be spiritually and morally qualified to be an elder. He may even be skilled in teaching and have a believing wife and children who follow his leadership in the home, but he can't seem to pull his finances into proper order. Since in the area of finances he doesn't rule his household well, he is disqualified from spiritual leadership. Stewardship of possessions is a critical test of a man's leadership. His home is a proving ground where his administrative capabilities can be clearly demonstrated.

In addition, a father must have enough love to make it easy for his children to obey him. Your children ought to long to obey you because they would never want to do anything that would hinder their relationship with you. There's no better place to see a man's commitment to meeting the needs of others than in his own home. Does he care about his family? Is he committed to each member? Does he work hard to meet their needs? If he doesn't, how could he ever care for the church?

Think:

Pray: (Add other specific requests.)

Day 21

Read: *This is a faithful saying: If a man desires the position of a bishop, he desires a good work. A bishop then must be* ***... not a novice lest being puffed up with pride he fall into the same condemnation as the devil.*** (1 Timothy 3:1, 6)

An elder should not be a new convert or newly baptized. The opposite of a new believer is a mature Christian. An elder must be mature in the faith. Of course maturity is relative, so the standard of maturity will vary from congregation to congregation. The point is that an elder must be more spiritually mature than the people he leads. "The condemnation of the devil" was a demotion from high position on account of pride. God will do the same to any man whose thinking is clouded with pride and whose perception of his own spirituality is distorted because of a premature rise to spiritual leadership.

Think:

Pray: (Add other specific requests.)

Day 22

Read: *This is a faithful saying: If a man desires the position of a bishop, he desires a good work. A bishop ...* ***must have a good testimony among those who are outside, lest he fall into reproach and the snare of the devil.*** (1 Timothy 3:1, 7)

An elder must have a good internal character and a good external reputation or testimony. Elders need a good reputation with those outside the church so they don't fall into "the snare of the devil." Satan tries to entrap spiritual leaders so that he might destroy their credibility and integrity. He's like a roaring lion seeking to devour (1 Pet. 5:8), and spiritual leaders are his primary target. Like all Christians, elders have areas of weakness and vulnerability, and they will sometimes fall into one of Satan's traps. Only a perfect man doesn't stumble (James 3:2). Elders must be particularly discerning and cautious to avoid the snares of the enemy. Then they can be effective in leading others away from his traps. The Ephesian church needed to examine its leaders, and we do as well. The future of the church depends on the quality of today's leaders. God is building men to lead His flock. As a church we must identify them, place them into leadership, pray for them, and follow their example. In so doing we will bring glory to God.

Think:

Pray: (Add other specific requests.)

Day 23

Paul prayerfully planted vital churches then he recruited these churches to pray for him so that he could plant more vital churches. Paul's prayers for the churches provide clues to what we should pray for our churches and his prayer requests give insight as to what we should pray for our church leaders.

Paul's Prayers

Read: *Therefore I also, after I heard of your faith in the Lord Jesus and your love for all the saints, do not cease to give thanks for you, making mention of you in my prayers: that the God of our Lord Jesus Christ, the Father of glory, may give to you the spirit of wisdom and revelation in the knowledge of Him, the eyes of your understanding being enlightened; that you may know what is the hope of His calling, what are the riches of the glory of His inheritance in the saints, and what is the exceeding greatness of His power toward us who believe, according to the working of His mighty power which He worked in Christ when He*

raised Him from the dead and seated Him at His right hand in the heavenly places, far above all principality and power and might and dominion, and every name that is named, not only in this age but also in that which is to come. And He put all things under His feet, and gave Him to be head over all things to the church, which is His body, the fullness of Him who fills all in all. (Ephesians 1:15-23)
Think:
Pray:

Day 24
Read: *For this reason I bow my knees to the Father of our Lord Jesus Christ, from whom the whole family in heaven and earth is named, that He would grant you, according to the riches of His glory, to be strengthened with might through His Spirit in the inner man, that Christ may dwell in your hearts through faith; that you, being rooted and grounded in love, may be able to comprehend with all the saints what is the width and length and depth and height--to know the love of Christ which passes knowledge; that you may be filled with all the fullness of God. Now to Him who is able to do exceedingly abundantly above all that we ask or think, according to the power that works in us, to Him be glory in the church by Christ Jesus to all generations, forever and ever. Amen.* (Ephesians 3:14-21)
Think:
Pray:

Day 25
Read: *Night and day praying exceedingly that we may see your face and perfect what is lacking in your faith?*

Now may our God and Father Himself, and our Lord Jesus Christ, direct our way to you. And may the Lord make you increase and abound in love to one another and

to all, just as we do to you, so that He may establish your hearts blameless in holiness before our God and Father at the coming of our Lord Jesus Christ with all His saints. (1 Thessalonians 3:10-13)
Think:
Pray:

Day 26
Read: *Rejoice always, pray without ceasing, in everything give thanks; for this is the will of God in Christ Jesus for you.* (1 Thessalonians 5:16-18)
Think:
Pray:

Day 27
Read: *Now may the God of peace Himself sanctify you completely; and may your whole spirit, soul, and body be preserved blameless at the coming of our Lord Jesus Christ. He who calls you is faithful, who also will do it. Brethren, pray for us…The grace of our Lord Jesus Christ be with you. Amen.* (1 Thessalonians 5:23-25; 28)
Think:
Pray:

Day 28
Read: *Therefore we also pray always for you that our God would count you worthy of this calling, and fulfill all the good pleasure of His goodness and the work of faith with power, that the name of our Lord Jesus Christ may be glorified in you, and you in Him, according to the grace of our God and the Lord Jesus Christ.* (2 Thess.1:11-12)
Think:
Pray:

Day 29

Read: *Now may the God of peace who brought up our Lord Jesus from the dead, that great Shepherd of the sheep, through the blood of the everlasting covenant, make you complete in every good work to do His will, working in you what is well pleasing in His sight, through Jesus Christ, to whom be glory forever and ever. Amen.* (Hebrews 13: 20-21)

Think:

Pray:

Paul's Prayer Requests

Day 30

Read: *Now I beg you, brethren, through the Lord Jesus Christ, and through the love of the Spirit, that you strive together with me in prayers to God for me, that I may be delivered from those in Judea who do not believe, and that my service for Jerusalem may be acceptable to the saints, that I may come to you with joy by the will of God, and may be refreshed together with you.* (Romans 15:30-32)

Think:

Pray:

Day 31

Read: *Praying always with all prayer and supplication in the Spirit, being watchful to this end with all perseverance and supplication for all the saints-- and for me, that utterance may be given to me, that I may open my mouth boldly to make known the mystery of the gospel, for which I am an ambassador in chains; that in it I may speak boldly, as I ought to speak.* (Ephesians 6:18-20)

Think:

Pray:

Day 32

Read: *But I want you to know, brethren, that the things which happened to me have actually turned out for the furtherance of the gospel, so that it has become evident to the whole palace guard, and to all the rest, that my chains are in Christ; and most of the brethren in the Lord, having become confident by my chains, are much more bold to speak the word without fear. Some indeed preach Christ even from envy and strife, and some also from good will: The former preach Christ from selfish ambition, not sincerely, supposing to add affliction to my chains; but the latter out of love, knowing that I am appointed for the defense of the gospel. What then? Only that in every way, whether in pretense or in truth, Christ is preached; and in this I rejoice, yes, and will rejoice. For I know that this will turn out for my deliverance through your prayer and the supply of the Spirit of Jesus Christ, according to my earnest expectation and hope that in nothing I shall be ashamed, but with all boldness, as always, so now also Christ will be magnified in my body, whether by life or by death.* (Philippians 1:12-20)

Think:

Pray:

Day 33

Read: *Finally, brethren, pray for us, that the word of the Lord may run swiftly and be glorified, just as it is with you, and that we may be delivered from unreasonable and wicked men; for not all have faith.*(2 Thessalonians 3:1-2)

Think:

Pray:

Day 34

Read: *Obey those who rule over you, and be submissive, for they watch out for your souls, as those who must give*

account. Let them do so with joy and not with grief, for that would be unprofitable for you.
Pray for us; for we are confident that we have a good conscience, in all things desiring to live honorably. But I especially urge you to do this, that I may be restored to you the sooner. (Hebrews 13: 17-19)
Think:
Pray:

Day 35
Read: *Continue earnestly in prayer, being vigilant in it with thanksgiving; meanwhile praying also for us, that God would open to us a door for the word, to speak the mystery of Christ, for which I am also in chains, that I may make it manifest, as I ought to speak.* (Col. 4:2-4)
Think:
Pray:

Day 36
Read: *Confess your trespasses to one another, and pray for one another, that you may be healed. The effective, fervent prayer of a righteous man avails much. Elijah was a man with a nature like ours, and he prayed earnestly that it would not rain; and it did not rain on the land for three years and six months. And he prayed again, and the heaven gave rain, and the earth produced its fruit.*
Brethren, if anyone among you wanders from the truth, and someone turns him back, let him know that he who turns a sinner from the error of his way will save a soul from death and cover a multitude of sins. (James 5:16-20)
Think:
Pray:

Day 37
Read: *Now it came to pass, as He was praying in a*

certain place, when He ceased, that one of His disciples said to Him, "Lord, teach us to pray, as John also taught his disciples." So He said to them, "When you pray, say:

Our Father in heaven,
Hallowed be Your name.
Your kingdom come.
Your will be done
On earth as it is in heaven.
Give us day by day our daily bread.
And forgive us our sins,
For we also forgive everyone who is indebted to us.
And do not lead us into temptation,
But deliver us from the evil one." (Luke 11:1-4)

Think:

Pray:

Day 38

Read: "Our Father in heaven"

I will be a Father to you, and you shall be My sons and daughters, says the Lord Almighty. For you did not receive the spirit of bondage again to fear, but you received the Spirit of adoption by whom we cry out, "Abba, Father." (2 Cor. 6:18; Romans 8:15)

Think:

Pray:

Day 39

Read: "Hallowed be Your name."

Who is like You, O Lord, among the gods? Who is like You, glorious in holiness, fearful in praises, doing wonders? Give unto the Lord the glory due to His name; worship the Lord in the beauty of holiness. For God did not call us to uncleanness, but in holiness. Pursue peace with all people, and holiness, without which no one will

see the Lord. (Exodus 15:11; Psalm 29:2; 1 Thes. 4:7; Hebrews 12:14)
Think:
Pray:

Day 40
***Read*: "*Your kingdom come.*"**
Jesus answered, "Most assuredly, I say to you, unless one is born of water and the Spirit, he cannot enter the kingdom of God .... But seek first the kingdom of God and His righteousness, and all these things shall be added to you".. For the kingdom of God is not eating and drinking, but righteousness and peace and joy in the Holy Spirit.... For the kingdom of God is not in word but in power...
Then I heard a loud voice saying in heaven, "Now salvation, and strength, and the kingdom of our God, and the power of His Christ have come, for the accuser of our brethren, who accused them before our God day and night, has been cast down"... "And the Lord will deliver me from every evil work and preserve me for His heavenly kingdom. To Him be glory forever and ever. Amen!" (John 3:5; Matthew 6:33; Romans 14:17; 1 Cor. 4:20; Rev. 12:10; 2 Tim. 4:18)
Think:
Pray:

Day 41
Read: "Your will be done on earth as it is in heaven."
For this is the will of God, your sanctification: that you should abstain from sexual immorality; In everything give thanks; for this is the will of God in Christ Jesus for you. For this is the will of God, that by doing good you may put to silence the ignorance of foolish men-- For you have need of endurance, so that after you have done the will of God, you may receive the promise. And the world is passing away, and the lust of it; but he who does the will

of God abides forever. (1 Thess. 4:3; 5:18; 1 Peter 2:15; Hebrews 10:36; 1 John 2:17)
Think:
Pray:

Day 42
***Read*: "*Give us day by day our daily bread.*"**
So He humbled you, allowed you to hunger, and fed you with manna which you did not know nor did your fathers know, that He might make you know that man shall not live by bread alone; but man lives by every word that proceeds from the mouth of the Lord. All the labor of man is for his mouth, and yet the soul is not satisfied. (Deut. 8:3; Eccles. 6:7)
Think:
Pray:

Day 43
Read: "And forgive us our sins, for we also forgive everyone who is indebted to us."
If My people who are called by My name will humble themselves, and pray and seek My face, and turn from their wicked ways, then I will hear from heaven, and will forgive their sin and heal their land. Take heed to yourselves. If your brother sins against you, rebuke him; and if he repents, forgive him. And if he sins against you seven times in a day, and seven times in a day returns to you, saying, 'I repent,' you shall forgive him." Then Jesus said, "Father, forgive them, for they do not know what they do." And they divided His garments and cast lots. If we confess our sins, He is faithful and just to forgive us our sins and to cleanse us from all unrighteousness. (2 Chron. 7:14; Luke 17:3-4; Luke 23:34; 1 John 1:9)
Think:
Pray:

Day 44

Read: "And do not lead us into temptation."

Watch and pray, lest you enter into temptation. The spirit indeed is willing, but the flesh is weak." No temptation has overtaken you except such as is common to man; but God is faithful, who will not allow you to be tempted beyond what you are able, but with the temptation will also make the way of escape, that you may be able to bear it. But those who desire to be rich fall into temptation and a snare, and into many foolish and harmful lusts which drown men in destruction and perdition. Blessed is the man who endures temptation; for when he has been approved, he will receive the crown of life which the Lord has promised to those who love Him. (Matthew 26:41; 1 Cor. 10:13; 1 Tim. 6:9; James 1:12)

Think:

Pray:

Day 45

Read: "But deliver us from the evil one."

I do not pray that You should take them out of the world, but that You should keep them from the evil one. But the Lord is faithful, who will establish you and guard you from the evil one. For this reason I also suffer these things; nevertheless I am not ashamed, for I know whom I have believed and am persuaded that He is able to keep what I have committed to Him until that Day. Now to Him who is able to keep you from stumbling, and to present you faultless before the presence of His glory with exceeding joy, to God our Savior, who alone is wise, be glory and majesty, dominion and power, both now and forever. Amen. (John 17:15; 2 Thes. 3:3; 2 Tim. 1:12; Jude 1:24, 25)

Think:

Pray:

Day 46
Read: *From Miletus he sent to Ephesus and called for the elders of the church. And when they had come to him, he said to them: "You know, from the first day that I came to Asia, in what manner I always lived among you, serving the Lord with all humility, with many tears and trials which happened to me by the plotting of the Jews; how I kept back nothing that was helpful, but proclaimed it to you, and taught you publicly and from house to house, testifying to Jews, and also to Greeks, repentance toward God and faith toward our Lord Jesus Christ*. (Acts 20:17-21)
Think:
Pray:

Day 47
Read: *And see, now I go bound in the spirit to Jerusalem, not knowing the things that will happen to me there, except that the Holy Spirit testifies in every city, saying that chains and tribulations await me. But none of these things move me; nor do I count my life dear to myself, so that I may finish my race with joy, and the ministry which I received from the Lord Jesus, to testify to the gospel of the grace of God*. (Acts 20:22-24)
Think:
Pray:

Day 48
Read: *And indeed, now I know that you all, among whom I have gone preaching the kingdom of God, will see my face no more. Therefore I testify to you this day that I am innocent of the blood of all men. For I have not shunned to declare to you the whole counsel of God.* (Acts 20:25-27).
Think:
Pray:

Day 49
Read: *Therefore take heed to yourselves and to all the flock, among which the Holy Spirit has made you overseers, to shepherd the church of God which He purchased with His own blood. For I know this, that after my departure savage wolves will come in among you, not sparing the flock. Also from among yourselves men will rise up, speaking perverse things, to draw away the disciples after themselves. Therefore watch, and remember that for three years I did not cease to warn everyone night and day with tears.*(Acts 20:28-31).
Think:
Pray:

Day 50
Read: *So now, brethren, I commend you to God and to the word of His grace, which is able to build you up and give you an inheritance among all those who are sanctified. I have coveted no one's silver or gold or apparel. Yes, you yourselves know that these hands have provided for my necessities, and for those who were with me. I have shown you in every way, by laboring like this, that you must support the weak. And remember the words of the Lord Jesus, that He said, "It is more blessed to give than to receive."* (Acts 20:32-35)
Think:
Pray:

Day 51
Read: *Jesus spoke these words, lifted up His eyes to heaven, and said: "Father, the hour has come. Glorify Your Son, that Your Son also may glorify You, as You have given Him authority over all flesh, that He should give eternal life to as many as You have given Him. And this is eternal life, that they may know You, the only true God,*

and Jesus Christ whom You have sent. I have glorified You on the earth. I have finished the work which You have given Me to do. And now, O Father, glorify Me together with Yourself, with the glory which I had with You before the world was." (John 17:1-5)
Think:
Pray:

Day 52
Read: *I have manifested Your name to the men whom You have given Me out of the world. They were Yours, You gave them to Me, and they have kept Your word. Now they have known that all things which You have given Me are from You. For I have given to them the words which You have given Me; and they have received them, and have known surely that I came forth from You; and they have believed that You sent Me. I pray for them. I do not pray for the world but for those whom You have given Me, for they are Yours. And all Mine are Yours, and Yours are Mine, and I am glorified in them*. (John 17:6-10)
Think:
Pray:

Day 53
Read: *Now I am no longer in the world, but these are in the world, and I come to You. Holy Father, keep through Your name those whom You have given Me, that they may be one as We are. While I was with them in the world, I kept them in Your name. Those whom You gave Me I have kept; and none of them is lost except the son of perdition, that the Scripture might be fulfilled. But now I come to You, and these things I speak in the world, that they may have My joy fulfilled in themselves*. (John 17:11-13)
Think:
Pray:

Day 54
Read: *I have given them Your word; and the world has hated them because they are not of the world, just as I am not of the world. I do not pray that You should take them out of the world, but that You should keep them from the evil one. They are not of the world, just as I am not of the world. Sanctify them by Your truth. Your word is truth. As You sent Me into the world, I also have sent them into the world. And for their sakes I sanctify Myself, that they also may be sanctified by the truth.* (John 17:14-19)
Think:
Pray:

Day 55
Read: *I do not pray for these alone, but also for those who will believe in Me through their word; that they all may be one, as You, Father, are in Me, and I in You; that they also may be one in Us, that the world may believe that You sent Me. And the glory which You gave Me I have given them, that they may be one just as We are one: I in them, and You in Me; that they may be made perfect in one, and that the world may know that You have sent Me, and have loved them as You have loved Me.* (John 17:20-23)
Think:
Pray:

Day 56
Read: *Father, I desire that they also whom You gave Me may be with Me where I am, that they may behold My glory which You have given Me; for You loved Me before the foundation of the world. O righteous Father! The world has not known You, but I have known You; and these have known that You sent Me. And I have declared to them Your name, and will declare it, that the love with*

which You loved Me may be in them, and I in them. (John 17:24-26)
Think:
Pray:

Day 57

Praying the Psalms

Sequentially read aloud through the verses of a Psalm. Then pray as the Holy Spirit prompts through the verse. This may be thanking God for the truth in the verse; it may be petition asking Him to enable you to do what the verse implies you should do. Your prayer may be intercession asking the Lord to do in another's life what the verse brings to your mind. In this situation, pray for your pastor and the leaders of your church. In Psalm One below, the bold sentences following each verse provide an example of this process.

Psalm 1:1-6 NKJ
Read: [1] *Blessed is the man who walks not in the counsel of the ungodly, nor stands in the path of sinners, nor sits in the seat of the scornful;*
Think:
Pray: **Father, bless my pastor, the leaders of my church, our missionaries and chaplains by enabling them not to follow evil men's advice, or hang around with sinners, scoffing at the things of God.**

Read: *[2] But his delight is in the law of the Lord, And in His law he meditates day and night.*
Think:
Pray: **Father, help my pastor, the leaders of my church, our missionaries and chaplains to delight in Your law, and to think night and day how they can more closely obey it.**

Read: *[3] He shall be like a tree Planted by the rivers of water, That brings forth its fruit in its season, Whose leaf also shall not wither; And whatever he does shall prosper.*
Think:
Pray: **Father, make my pastor, the leaders of my church, our missionaries and chaplains like trees with a river of never-ending water, trees that bear luscious fruit each season without fail. Keep them from spiritual drought and enable them to prosper in all You give them to do.**

Read: *[4] The ungodly are not so, But are like the chaff which the wind drives away.*
Think:
Pray: **Father, You declare that sinners, will blow away like chaff before the wind. May Your Spirit, like the wind, blow upon us and remove all the chaff of wickedness from me, my pastor, the leaders of my church, our missionaries and chaplains.**

Read: *[5] Therefore the ungodly shall not stand in the judgment, nor sinners in the congregation of the righteous.*
Think:
Pray: **Father, I thank You that through the righteousness of Christ, I know my pastor, the leaders of my church, our missionaries and chaplains, and I will be safe on Judgment Day. They will stand among the godly.**

Read: *[6] For the Lord knows the way of the righteous, but the way of the ungodly shall perish.*
Think:
Pray: **Father, I thank You that You watch over all the plans and paths of my pastor, the leaders of my church,**

our missionaries and chaplains, keep them from the godless paths that lead to doom.

Day 58
Read: A Psalm of David.
The Lord is my shepherd; I shall not want. He makes me to lie down in green pastures; He leads me beside the still waters. He restores my soul; He leads me in the paths of righteousness for His name's sake. (Psalm 23:1-3)
Think:
Pray:

Day 59
Read: *Yea, though I walk through the valley of the shadow of death, I will fear no evil; for You are with me; Your rod and Your staff, they comfort me.* (Psalm 23:4)
Think:
Pray:

Day 60
Read: *You prepare a table before me in the presence of my enemies; You anoint my head with oil; my cup runs over. Surely goodness and mercy shall follow me all the days of my life; and I will dwell in the house of the Lord Forever.* (Psalm 23:5-6)
Think:
Pray:

Additional New Testament Prayers

So when they heard that, they raised their voice to God with one accord and said: "Lord, You are God, who made heaven and earth and the sea, and all that is in them, who by the mouth of Your servant David have said: 'Why did the nations rage, and the people plot vain things? The

kings of the earth took their stand, and the rulers were gathered together against the Lord and against His Christ.' "
"For truly against Your holy Servant Jesus, whom You anointed, both Herod and Pontius Pilate, with the Gentiles and the people of Israel, were gathered together to do whatever Your hand and Your purpose determined before to be done. Now, Lord, look on their threats, and grant to Your servants that with all boldness they may speak Your word, by stretching out Your hand to heal, and that signs and wonders may be done through the name of Your holy Servant Jesus." (Acts 4:24-30)

For I could wish that I myself were cursed and cut off from Christ for the sake of my brothers, those of my own race....Brothers, my heart's desire and prayer to God for the Israelites is that they may be saved. (Romans 9:3; 10:1 NIV)

Now may the God of hope fill you with all joy and peace in believing, that you may abound in hope by the power of the Holy Spirit. ...Now the God of peace be with you all. Amen. (Romans 15:13, 33)

Now to Him who is able to establish you according to my gospel and the preaching of Jesus Christ, according to the revelation of the mystery kept secret since the world began but now has been made manifest, and by the prophetic Scriptures has been made known to all nations, according to the commandment of the everlasting God, for obedience to the faith-- to God, alone wise, be glory through Jesus Christ forever. Amen. (Romans 16:25-27)

Grace to you and peace from God our Father and the Lord Jesus Christ. Blessed be the God and Father of our Lord Jesus Christ, the Father of mercies and God of all comfort, who comforts us in all our tribulation, that we may be able to comfort those who are in any trouble, with the comfort with which we ourselves are comforted by God. (2 Corinthians 1:2-4)

But thanks be to God, who always leads us in triumphal procession in Christ and through us spreads everywhere the fragrance of the knowledge of him. (2 Cor. 2:14 NIV)

And this is my prayer: that your love may abound more and more in knowledge and depth of insight, so that you may be able to discern what is best and may be pure and blameless until the day of Christ, filled with the fruit of righteousness that comes through Jesus Christ--to the glory and praise of God. (Philippians 1:9-11 NIV)

For this reason we also, since the day we heard it, do not cease to pray for you, and to ask that you may be filled with the knowledge of His will in all wisdom and spiritual understanding; that you may walk worthy of the Lord, fully pleasing Him, being fruitful in every good work and increasing in the knowledge of God; strengthened with all might, according to His glorious power, for all patience and longsuffering with joy; giving thanks to the Father who has qualified us to be partakers of the inheritance of the saints in the light. (Colossians 1:9-12)

For this reason we also thank God without ceasing, because when you received the word of God which you heard from us, you welcomed it not as the word of men, but as it is in truth, the word of God, which also effectively works in you who believe. (1 Thessalonians 2:13)

But we are bound to give thanks to God always for you, brethren beloved by the Lord, because God from the beginning chose you for salvation through sanctification by the Spirit and belief in the truth, to which He called you by our gospel, for the obtaining of the glory of our Lord Jesus Christ. (2 Thessalonians 2:13-14)

Now may our Lord Jesus Christ Himself, and our God and Father, who has loved us and given us everlasting consolation and good hope by grace, comfort your hearts and establish you in every good word and work. (2 Thessalonians 2:16-17)

Now may the Lord direct your hearts into the love of God and into the patience of Christ. ...Now may the Lord of peace Himself give you peace always in every way. ...The Lord be with you all. The grace of our Lord Jesus Christ be with you all. Amen. (2 Thessalonians 3:5, 16, 18)

Now to the King eternal, immortal, invisible, to God who alone is wise, be honor and glory forever and ever. Amen. (1 Timothy 1:17)

Grace to you and peace from God our Father and the Lord Jesus Christ. I thank my God, making mention of you always in my prayers, hearing of your love and faith which you have toward the Lord Jesus and toward all the saints, that the sharing of your faith may become effective by the acknowledgment of every good thing which is in you in Christ Jesus. (Philemon 1:3-6)

Now may the God of peace who brought up our Lord Jesus from the dead, that great Shepherd of the sheep, through the blood of the everlasting covenant, make you complete in every good work to do His will, working in you what is well pleasing in His sight, through Jesus Christ, to whom be glory forever and ever. Amen. (Hebrews 13:20-21)

But may the God of all grace, who called us to His eternal glory by Christ Jesus, after you have suffered a while, perfect, establish, strengthen, and settle you. To Him be the glory and the dominion forever and ever. Amen. (1 Peter 5:10-11)

Grace and peace be multiplied to you in the knowledge of God and of Jesus our Lord. (2 Peter 1:2)

Beloved, I pray that you may prosper in all things and be in health, just as your soul prospers. (3 John 1:2)

The four living creatures, each having six wings, were full of eyes around and within. And they do not rest day or night, saying: "Holy, holy, holy, Lord God Almighty, who was and is and is to come! ...You are worthy, O Lord, to receive glory and honor and power; for You created all things, and by Your will they exist and were created." (Revelation 4:8, 11)

And they sang a new song, saying: "You are worthy to take the scroll, and to open its seals; for You were slain, and have redeemed us to God by Your blood out of every tribe and tongue and people and nation, and have made us kings and priests to our God; and we shall reign on the earth."
Then I looked, and I heard the voice of many angels around the throne, the living creatures, and the elders;

and the number of them was ten thousand times ten thousand, and thousands of thousands, saying with a loud voice: "Worthy is the Lamb who was slain to receive power and riches and wisdom, and strength and honor and glory and blessing!" And every creature which is in heaven and on the earth and under the earth and such as are in the sea, and all that are in them, I heard saying: "Blessing and honor and glory and power be to Him who sits on the throne, and to the Lamb, forever and ever!" (Revelation 5:9-13)

"Salvation belongs to our God who sits on the throne, and to the Lamb!" All the angels stood around the throne and the elders and the four living creatures, and fell on their faces before the throne and worshiped God, saying: "Amen! Blessing and glory and wisdom, thanksgiving and honor and power and might, be to our God forever and ever. Amen." (Revelation 7:10-12)

Then the seventh angel sounded: And there were loud voices in heaven, saying, "The kingdoms of this world have become the kingdoms of our Lord and of His Christ, and He shall reign forever and ever!" And the twenty-four elders who sat before God on their thrones fell on their faces and worshiped God, saying: "We give You thanks, O Lord God Almighty, the One who is and who was and who is to come, because You have taken Your great power and reigned. The nations were angry, and Your wrath has come, and the time of the dead, that they should be judged, and that You should reward Your servants the prophets and the saints, and those who fear Your name, small and great, and should destroy those who destroy the earth." (Revelation 11:15-18)

After these things I heard a loud voice of a great multitude in heaven, saying, "Alleluia! Salvation and glory and honor and power belong to the Lord our God! For true and righteous are His judgments, because He has judged the great harlot who corrupted the earth with her fornication; and He has avenged on her the blood of His servants shed by her." Again they said, "Alleluia! Her smoke rises up forever and ever!" And the twenty-four elders and the four living creatures fell down and worshiped God who sat on the throne, saying, "Amen! Alleluia!" Then a voice came from the throne, saying, "Praise our God, all you His servants and those who fear Him, both small and great!" And I heard, as it were, the voice of a great multitude, as the sound of many waters and as the sound of mighty thunderings, saying, "Alleluia! For the Lord God Omnipotent reigns! Let us be glad and rejoice and give Him glory, for the marriage of the Lamb has come, and His wife has made herself ready." And to her it was granted to be arrayed in fine linen, clean and bright, for the fine linen is the righteous acts of the saints. (Revelation 19:1-8)

He who testifies to these things says, "Surely I am coming quickly." Amen. Even so, come, Lord Jesus! The grace of our Lord Jesus Christ be with you all. Amen. (Revelation 22:20-21)

Appendix Three

Prayer Guide to Discover and Develop Spiritual Gifts

This prayer guide is designed to encourage members of the local church to discover and develop their spiritual gifts. As you pray, remember that ministry is not only what you do at the church building. Normal daily work is ministry—when it is done in response to God's call and with eternal perspective. Find your name in your church directory and then begin to pray for the person whose name follows yours. Pray for this person each day for thirty days.

As the human body ages, it may suffer from hardening of the arteries. As local churches age, they may suffer from hardening of the categories. Institutionalism leads people to doing things habitually rather than because they are the most functional. When leaders pray and are prayed for, they are more likely to remain open to the fresh ministry of the Holy Spirit which is what keeps the church vigorous.

When a church understands that it is the people of God and that it exists to faithfully continue Christ's mission, it will not get diverted into secondary issues. One way a church participates in Christ's mission is by interceding for its missionaries. The truth of the matter is that a church that does not financially and prayerfully support missionaries is no church at all. The church that shines the greatest distance will also shine the brightest at home. As you pray for your local church leaders, include your missionaries. I also urge you to adopt a military chaplain. These people are on the cutting edge of evangelistic ministry.

Day 61

Read: *As each one has received a gift, minister it to one another, as good stewards of the manifold grace of God.* (1 Peter 4:10)

Think:

Pray: Father, enable me and those for whom I pray (insert names) to know and use the spiritual gifts You have given us to understand better what it means to be Your people and faithfully continue Christ's mission on earth.

> Because of the importance of the truth in 1 Peter 4:10, I urge you to write it on a card and carry it with you this month. Frequently each day, read aloud the words of this verse and ask God to make you and those for whom you pray to be faithful stewards.

Day 62

Read: *There are diversities of gifts, but the same Spirit. There are differences of ministries, but the same Lord. And there are diversities of activities, but it is the same God who works all in all. But the manifestation of the Spirit is given to each one for the profit of all. Examine yourselves to see if your faith is really genuine.* (1 Corinthians 12:4-7; 2 Corinthians 13:5)

Think:

Pray: Father, You give spiritual gifts to each of Your people as a means of helping the entire church. Help me and the people for whom I pray (insert names) to examine ourselves to see if our faith is genuine as determined by our proper use of the gifts You have given to each of us.

Day 63

Read: *But without faith it is impossible to please Him, for he who comes to God must believe that He is, and that He is a rewarder of those who diligently seek Him. God also bearing witness both with signs and wonders, with various miracles, and gifts of the Holy Spirit, according to His own will?* (Hebrews 11:6; 2:4)

Think:

Pray: Father, give me and those for whom I pray (insert names), faith to believe that you have given specific spiritual gifts to us.

Day 64

Read: *For we are His workmanship, created in Christ Jesus for good works, which God prepared beforehand that we should walk in them.* (Ephesians 2:10)

Think:

Pray: Father, I and those for whom I pray (insert names) are Your workmanship, created in Christ Jesus for good works, which You prepared beforehand that we should walk in them. Enable us to be Your people and faithfully continue Christ's mission in this world.

Day 65

Read: *If any of you lacks wisdom, let him ask of God, who gives to all liberally and without reproach, and it will be given to him.* (James 1:5)

Think:

Pray: Father, I and those for whom I pray, (insert names) need wisdom in using your gifts. You promised to give us wisdom when we ask in faith and do not doubt, so grant us this wisdom now.

Day 66

Read: *But the end of all things is at hand; therefore be serious and watchful in your prayers. And above all things have fervent love for one another, for "love will cover a multitude of sins." Be hospitable to one another without grumbling. As each one has received a gift, minister it to one another, as good stewards of the manifold grace of God. If anyone speaks, let him speak as the oracles of God. If anyone ministers, let him do it as with the ability which God supplies, that in all things God may be glorified through Jesus Christ, to whom belong the glory and the dominion forever and ever. Amen.* (1 Peter 4:7-11)

Think:

Pray: (From this point forward, wherever you see the instruction to pray, ask the Holy Spirit to enable you to turn your thinking on the daily verses into prayer and then pray by name for yourself and those on your prayer list.

Day 67

Read: *I beseech you therefore, brethren, by the mercies of God, that you present your bodies a living sacrifice, holy, acceptable to God, which is your reasonable service. And do not be conformed to this world, but be transformed by the renewing of your mind, that you may prove what is that good and acceptable and perfect will of God.* (Romans 12:1-2)

Think:

Pray:

Day 68

Read: *For I say, through the grace given to me, to everyone who is among you, not to think of himself more highly than he ought to think, but to think soberly, as God has dealt to each one a measure of faith. For as we have many members in one body, but all the members do not* *have the same function, so we, being many, are one body in Christ, and individually members of one another. Having then gifts differing according to the grace that is given to us, let us use them: if prophecy, let us prophesy in proportion to our faith; or ministry, let us use it in our ministering; he who teaches, in teaching; he who exhorts, in exhortation; he who gives, with liberality; he who leads, with diligence; he who shows mercy, with cheerfulness.* (Romans 12:3-8)

Think:

Pray:

Day 69

Read: *Now concerning spiritual gifts, brethren, I do not want you to be ignorant: You know that you were Gentiles, carried away to these dumb idols, however you were led. Therefore I make known to you that no one speaking by the Spirit of God calls Jesus accursed, and no one can say that Jesus is Lord except by the Holy Spirit. There are diversities of gifts, but the same Spirit. There are differences of ministries, but the same Lord. And there are diversities of activities, but it is the same God who works all in all. But the manifestation of the Spirit is given to each one for the profit of all.* (1 Corinthians 12:1-7)

Think:

Pray:

Day 70

Read: *For to one is given the word of wisdom through the Spirit, to another the word of knowledge through the same Spirit, to another faith by the same Spirit, to another gifts of healings by the same Spirit, to another the working of miracles, to another prophecy, to another discerning of spirits, to another different kinds of tongues, to another the interpretation of tongues. But one and the same Spirit*

works all these things, distributing to each one individually as He wills.
For as the body is one and has many members, but all the members of that one body, being many, are one body, so also is Christ. For by one Spirit we were all baptized into one body--whether Jews or Greeks, whether slaves or free-and have all been made to drink into one Spirit. (1 Corinthians 12:8-13)
Think:
Pray:

Day 71
Read: *For in fact the body is not one member but many. If the foot should say, "Because I am not a hand, I am not of the body," is it therefore not of the body? And if the ear should say, "Because I am not an eye, I am not of the body," is it therefore not of the body? If the whole body were an eye, where would be the hearing? If the whole were hearing, where would be the smelling? But now God has set the members, each one of them, in the body just as He pleased. And if they were all one member, where would the body be? But now indeed there are many members, yet one body. And the eye cannot say to the hand, "I have no need of you"; nor again the head to the feet, "I have no need of you." No, much rather, those members of the body which seem to be weaker are necessary. And those members of the body which we think to be less honorable, on these we bestow greater honor; and our unpresentable parts have greater modesty, but our presentable parts have no need.* (1 Corinthians 12:14-24)
Think:
Pray:

Day 72

Read: *But God composed the body, having given greater honor to that part which lacks it, that there should be no schism in the body, but that the members should have the same care for one another. And if one member suffers, all the members suffer with it; or if one member is honored, all the members rejoice with it. Now you are the body of Christ, and members individually. And God has appointed these in the church: first apostles, second prophets, third teachers, after that miracles, then gifts of healings, helps, administrations, varieties of tongues. Are all apostles? Are all prophets? Are all teachers? Are all workers of miracles? Do all have gifts of healings? Do all speak with tongues? Do all interpret? But earnestly desire the best gifts. And yet I show you a more excellent way.* (1 Corinthians 12:24-31)

Think:

Pray:

Day 73

Read: *Though I speak with the tongues of men and of angels, but have not love, I have become sounding brass or a clanging cymbal. And though I have the gift of prophecy, and understand all mysteries and all knowledge, and though I have all faith, so that I could remove mountains, but have not love, I am nothing. And though I bestow all my goods to feed the poor, and though I give my body to be burned, but have not love, it profits me nothing. Love suffers long and is kind; love does not envy; love does not parade itself, is not puffed up; does not behave rudely, does not seek its own, is not provoked, thinks no evil; does not rejoice in iniquity, but rejoices in the truth; bears all things, believes all things, hopes all things, endures all things. Love never fails. But whether there are prophecies, they will fail; whether there are tongues, they* *will cease; whether there is knowledge, it will vanish away. For we know in part and we prophesy in part. But when that which is perfect has come, then that which is in part will be done away.* (1 Corinthians 13:1-10)

Think:

Pray:

Day 74

Read: *When I was a child, I spoke as a child, I understood as a child, I thought as a child; but when I became a man, I put away childish things. For now we see in a mirror, dimly, but then face to face. Now I know in part, but then I shall know just as I also am known. And now abide faith, hope, love, these three; but the greatest of these is love. Pursue love, and desire spiritual gifts, but especially that you may prophesy. For he who speaks in a tongue does not speak to men but to God, for no one understands him; however, in the spirit he speaks mysteries. But he who prophesies speaks edification and exhortation and comfort to men. He who speaks in a tongue edifies himself, but he who prophesies edifies the church. I wish you all spoke with tongues, but even more that you prophesied; for he who prophesies is greater than he who speaks with tongues, unless indeed he interprets, that the church may receive edification.* (1 Corinthians 13:11-14, 5)

Think:

Pray:

Day 75

Read: *But now, brethren, if I come to you speaking with tongues, what shall I profit you unless I speak to you either by revelation, by knowledge, by prophesying, or by teaching? Even things without life, whether flute or harp, when they make a sound, unless they make a distinction in the sounds, how will it be known what is piped or played?*

For if the trumpet makes an uncertain sound, who will prepare himself for battle? So likewise you, unless you utter by the tongue words easy to understand, how will it be known what is spoken? For you will be speaking into the air. There are, it may be, so many kinds of languages in the world, and none of them is without significance. Therefore, if I do not know the meaning of the language, I shall be a foreigner to him who speaks, and he who speaks will be a foreigner to me. Even so you, since you are zealous for spiritual gifts, let it be for the edification of the church that you seek to excel. (1 Corinthians 14:6-12)
Think:
Pray:

Day 76
Read: *Therefore let him who speaks in a tongue pray that he may interpret. For if I pray in a tongue, my spirit prays, but my understanding is unfruitful. What is the conclusion then? I will pray with the spirit, and I will also pray with the understanding. I will sing with the spirit, and I will also sing with the understanding. Otherwise, if you bless with the spirit, how will he who occupies the place of the uninformed say "Amen" at your giving of thanks, since he does not understand what you say? For you indeed give thanks well, but the other is not edified. I thank my God I speak with tongues more than you all; yet in the church I would rather speak five words with my understanding, that I may teach others also, than ten thousand words in a tongue.* (1 Corinthians 14:13-19)
Think:
Pray:

***Day** 77*

Read: *Brethren, do not be children in understanding; however, in malice be babes, but in understanding be mature. In the law it is written:*

"With men of other tongues and other lips I will speak to this people; and yet, for all that, they will not hear Me," says the Lord. Therefore tongues are for a sign, not to those who believe but to unbelievers; but prophesying is not for unbelievers but for those who believe. Therefore if the whole church comes together in one place, and all speak with tongues, and there come in those who are uninformed or unbelievers, will they not say that you are out of your mind? But if all prophesy, and an unbeliever or an uninformed person comes in, he is convinced by all, he is convicted by all. And thus the secrets of his heart are revealed; and so, falling down on his face, he will worship God and report that God is truly among you. (1 Corinthians 14:19-25)

Think:

Pray:

Day 78

Read: *How is it then, brethren? Whenever you come together, each of you has a psalm, has a teaching, has a tongue, has a revelation, has an interpretation. Let all things be done for edification. If anyone speaks in a tongue, let there be two or at the most three, each in turn, and let one interpret. But if there is no interpreter, let him keep silent in church, and let him speak to himself and to God. Let two or three prophets speak, and let the others judge. But if anything is revealed to another who sits by, let the first keep silent.* (1 Corinthians 14: 26-29)

Think:

Pray:

Day 79
Read: *For you can all prophesy one by one, that all may learn and all may be encouraged. And the spirits of the prophets are subject to the prophets. For God is not the author of confusion but of peace, as in all the churches of the saints. Let your women keep silent in the churches, for they are not permitted to speak; but they are to be submissive, as the law also says. And if they want to learn something, let them ask their own husbands at home; for it is shameful for women to speak in church. Or did the word of God come originally from you? Or was it you only that it reached?* (1 Corinthians 14: 31-36)
Think:
Pray:

Day 80
Read: *If anyone thinks himself to be a prophet or spiritual, let him acknowledge that the things which I write to you are the commandments of the Lord. But if anyone is ignorant, let him be ignorant. Therefore, brethren, desire earnestly to prophesy, and do not forbid to speak with tongues.* (1 Corinthians 14:37-39)
Think:
Pray:

Day 81
Read: *I, therefore, the prisoner of the Lord, beseech you to walk worthy of the calling with which you were called, with all lowliness and gentleness, with longsuffering, bearing with one another in love, endeavoring to keep the unity of the Spirit in the bond of peace. There is one body and one Spirit, just as you were called in one hope of your calling; one Lord, one faith, one baptism; one God and Father of all, who is above all, and through all, and in you all.* (Ephesians 4:1-6)

Think
Pray:

Day 82
Read:
Grace to you and peace from God our Father and the Lord Jesus Christ. I thank my God always concerning you for the grace of God which was given to you by Christ Jesus, that you were enriched in everything by Him in all utterance and all knowledge, even as the testimony of Christ was confirmed in you, so that you come short in no gift, eagerly waiting for the revelation of our Lord Jesus Christ, who will also confirm you to the end, that you may be blameless in the day of our Lord Jesus Christ. God is faithful, by whom you were called into the fellowship of His Son, Jesus Christ our Lord. (1 Corinthians 1:3-9)
Think:
Pray:

Day 83
Read: *But to each one of us grace was given according to the measure of Christ's gift. Therefore He says:*

> *"When He ascended on high, He led captivity captive, and gave gifts to men."*

(Now this, "He ascended"--what does it mean but that He also first descended into the lower parts of the earth? He who descended is also the One who ascended far above all the heavens, that He might fill all things.) (Eph. 4:7-10)
Think:
Pray:

Day 84
Read: *And He Himself gave some to be apostles, some prophets, some evangelists, and some pastors and teachers, for the equipping of the saints for the work of*

ministry, for the edifying of the body of Christ, till we all come to the unity of the faith and of the knowledge of the Son of God, to a perfect man, to the measure of the stature of the fullness of Christ; that we should no longer be children, tossed to and fro and carried about with every wind of doctrine, by the trickery of men, in the cunning craftiness of deceitful plotting, but, speaking the truth in love, may grow up in all things into Him who is the head-- Christ-- from whom the whole body, joined and knit together by what every joint supplies, according to the effective working by which every part does its share, causes growth of the body for the edifying of itself in love. (Ephesians 4:11-16)
Think:
Pray:

Day 85
Read: *"Moreover it is required in stewards that one be found faithful."* (1 Corinthians 4:2)
Think:
Pray:

Day 86
Read: *As each one has received a gift, minister it to one another, as good stewards of the manifold grace of God. If anyone speaks, let him speak as the oracles of God. If anyone ministers, let him do it as with the ability which God supplies, that in all things God may be glorified through Jesus Christ, to whom belong the glory and the dominion forever and ever. Amen.* (1 Peter 4:10-11)
Think:
Pray:

Day 87
Read: "Each member of the local church – young or old, male or female, educated or uneducated, rich or poor– is viewed as a living stone in a cathedral for Christ's praise and presence. Brick buildings require that each block be cast from the same mold to fit together smoothly. But, in a 'living stone' cathedral, each person is unique. God is building us into a living community with Christ as the Master builder."
Think:
Pray:

Day 88
Read: "The Bible lists both 'ordinary' and 'extraordinary' spiritual gifts. Sincere Christians have disagreed on the nature of the 'sign and wonder' gifts after the time of the Apostles (2 Corinthians 12:12). Truly the signs of an apostle were accomplished among you with all perseverance, in signs and wonders and mighty deeds." It is important to say that SOME GIFTS are confirming signs to reveal Jesus Christ to the world, in His Person and written Word. But ALL GIFTS are given to enable His Body to reflect Him to the world. Jesus becomes real to the world when His praise and presence are embodied in a community of gifted, loving believers who serve others in His Name. Therefore, YOUR GIFTS, whether public or private, up-front or behind the scenes, are indispensable to help complete a picture of Jesus Christ to our world today.
Think:
Pray:

Day 89
Read: *But now indeed there are many members, yet one body. And the eye cannot say to the hand, "I have no need of you"; nor again the head to the feet, "I have no need of*

you." No, much rather, those members of the body which seem to be weaker are necessary. And those members of the body which we think to be less honorable, on these we bestow greater honor; and our unpresentable parts have greater modesty, but our presentable parts have no need. But God composed the body, having given greater honor to that part which lacks it, that there should be no schism in the body, but that the members should have the same care for one another. (1 Corinthians 12:20-25)
Think:
Pray:

Day 90
Read: *As you come to Him, the living Stone ... you also, like living stones, are being built into a spiritual house...* (1 Peter 2:5) January begins the calendar year and is a good time for the whole local church to declare its dependence on God by extraordinary prayer.
Think:
Pray:

Appendix Four

Starting Prayerwalking

For a description of what Prayerwalking is read page 121. The following guidelines will help you start and maintain an effective ministry of prayerwalking.

• **Prayerwalk with other believers.** Join your faith with others to help prayer flow in an engaging conversational style. Pairs work best; large groups decrease individual participation. Family prayerwalking is an exception to this rule and it provides an exciting variation for family worship, especially with small children.

• **Set aside time.** Periodically, e.g., once a month church members should gather at the church building for Prayerwalking the church target area. Plan to invest one to two full hours; begin with a time of brief instruction and prayer for the day's activity. Then pair up and go to your assigned area and prayerwalk. Return to the church at the agreed upon time for sharing and final prayer. For those who have never prayerwalked before, this is best way to begin the discipline.

In addition to prayerwalking the church neighborhood, plan to spend at least fifteen minutes once a week to Prayerwalk your residential neighborhood.

• **Choose an area.** Ask God to guide you. It's best to first learn the joys of prayerwalking in your church neighborhood. Inexperienced people gain confidence by joining forces with experienced Prayerwalkers. Then you return quickly to your own neighborhood with fresh vision. Centers of commerce and religion are fascinating, but there's nothing like touching families, schools and churches in residential areas. Use elevated points to pray over a panorama. Frequently, I go to the Sun Dial, a revolving restaurant on the 73rd floor of the Weston Hotel in the Atlanta midtown. In one hour the restaurant makes one full revolution, providing a 360-degree view of the whole city. I spend this hour praying for the Spirit to conquer the city. Linger at specific sties that seem to be strategic.

• **Pray with Insight.** Pray for people you see. As you do, the Spirit of God will calibrate your heart with His own sensitivities. Enhance these responsive insights with research done beforehand. Use knowledge of past events and current trends to enrich intercession. Above all, pray Scripture. Select just about any biblical prayers, and you will find that they almost pray themselves. Paul's words in 1 Timothy 2:1-5 is a good place to begin.

• **Focus on God.** Make God's promises rather than Satan's schemes the highlight of your prayers. Seek a restraining order from heaven upon evil so that God's empowered people may bring forth God's intended blessings on the city.

• **Gather and report.** Share what you experience and pray both in your home and around the church. Expressing something of your insights and faith will encourage others, as well as yourself. Set plans for further prayerwalking.

• **Target Strongholds.** This should include schools, hospitals, clinics, abortion clinics, strip clubs, porn shops, jails, prisons, high crime areas and poverty pockets. Like Elijah on Mount Carmel, attack the devil on his own ground![328] Also give high priority to areas of ethnic diversity from the majority of the present members of your congregation.

• **Coordinate efforts.** Enlist other praying people to join with you to cover special areas. Give leadership by forming and mixing prayer bands. Seek to collect written notes recording which areas have been covered and what kinds of prayers have been prayed. Pool your insights to ascertain whether God is prompting a repeated focus on particular area. Eventually aim to cover your entire town or city, unless God guides otherwise.

---

[328] 1 Kings 18:17-40

Appendix Five

How to Pray for Missionaries

Ron Shaw
Director of Spiritual Life
Mission to the World

Since my wife, Queta and I have spent a lot of time with missionaries on the field in the past several years, I would like to share with you some features of missionary life that will help you to pray more intelligently and effectively.

1. Physical well-being and safety of missionaries and their families

Missionaries, especially in the two thirds world, can be exposed to diseases that are particularly devastating, such as malaria, (from which more than one million people in Africa die every year) hepatitis, parasites and illnesses which come from sources such as dirty water. The water often must be filtered and boiled before it can be drunk. Sometimes the only place to purchase meats will be stores and open markets which have no refrigeration. Even vegetables, because they may have been fertilized with human excrement or heavily sprayed with unhealthy chemicals, will have to be carefully washed in a Clorox solution before they are eaten. Missionaries and their families in the developing world may also be exposed to outbreaks of illnesses such as typhus, meningitis, cholera or even plague. Health care in case of the need for emergency surgery or special medications may be very inadequate. There are also environmental health concerns. For example, in many of the world's major cities, e. g. Mexico City one of the largest cities in the world with about 25,000,000 people, air pollution is a very serious problem which results in health hazards ranging from elevated lead levels in the blood from the use of leaded gasoline to breathing air laden with sewage particulates.

Some of our missionaries have been abducted and robbed or their homes have been invaded for the purpose of robbery. In the past it has been unusual for such break-ins to be accompanied with the threat of violence, but it is now becoming more common. Some of our missionaries are in places very unfriendly to Christianity and to Americans in particular. Some of our missionaries have been through civil wars or armed strife in the regions where they live. Often driving in much of the world is by our standards much more chaotic and also more dangerous. Missionaries are sometimes exposed routinely to danger in travel or to the possibility of hitting and injuring or even killing a pedestrian. People in much of the world walk very close to or on the road and just do not seem to have an understanding of how devastating it is when a person is struck by a car. If a missionary should hit and kill a pedestrian, the legal and social consequences can be very serious. A missionary could be put in jail or have to pay a heavy fine or be forced to leave the country even though it was not his fault.

Adequate, safe, affordable housing which is appropriate and which promotes ministry is also important. In addition, finding a reliable automobile for an affordable price and then finding parts and a competent and honest repair shop can also be a tremendous problem. Pray for all of these kinds of needs for your missionaries, but most of all pray for them to have a bold and joyful witness when the Lord withholds these temporal "necessities".

2. Marriage and Family Life

Are missionaries such super spiritual people that they are not tempted to immorality or sexual lust? We all know the answer to that question. I think that one of the reasons that the church does not pray for missionaries is that it has put them on an unrealistic spiritual pedestal where they do not deserve to be and from which they may fall. Missionaries are ordinary Christians with an extraordinary Divine calling for which they need God's grace and power in Christ both personally and professionally. They serve on the front lines of spiritual war where they are are subject to the assaults of the evil one, and when they fall in their marriages, it is particularly devastating to them, their families and the gospel.

There are cultures in which pornography is much more open and easily available, e.g. on news stands and TV, and where behavior and dress are more provocative even than in the US, and this especially will constitute a temptation to male missionaries. Of course internet pornography is becoming an increasing temptation both for the church in America and around the world, and our men on the field are not exempt from this temptation. Pray that your missionaries will have a commitment to a regular day off, that they will take their yearly vacation time and that husbands and wives will spend time together on a regular basis to nurture their relationship. It will be difficult to do these things because of the press of ministry responsibilities. Missionaries are also very careful about how they use their supporters' money, and no missionary has money in great supply. As their supporters, encourage your missionaries to take some money occasionally for dates or vacation. Pray for quality and quantity time together for husband and wife. A wife can sometimes feel neglected on the field because her husband is so wholeheartedly dedicated to his ministry that he sometimes forgets about his wife and children and their needs. The wife on the other hand may be "stuck at home" with the kids, not as involved in ministry and meeting others or learning language as rapidly as her husband. She may also for the first time in her life be dealing with and trying to manage a house helper. Having stated these concerns, let me also say that missionary marriages and families are among the most solid in the church, and that it is this health in their marriages and families that results in a compelling testimony to those in the cultures where they serve.

Missionaries, especially those who are in their third or fourth term, may be dealing with the reality of **aging and infirm parents** in the States and they feel caught between two competing and equally important responsibilities: God's call on their lives and God's command to take care of their parents. Pray for the ability to see things clearly and for wisdom from the Lord in this matter of parental care. A missionary is often faced with this issue at the time of their greatest productivity.

3. For MKs (missionary kids)

Missionary kids, part of that group called Third Culture Kids, have many special challenges and opportunities. They have a passport country and an adopted country. Soon their adopted country is going to be very much their home, and America, their passport country, will become increasingly foreign to them. MKs have many things going for them and by and large tend to be very healthy emotionally and socially and spiritually. They are usually bright, adaptable, creative, possess strong cross-cultural skills, have had a variety of experiences and are fairly unworldly in the good sense. Missionary families tend to be close knit and MKs usually relate well to adults.

Pray about the issues of schooling. Will it be home schooling, public school, private Christian school, a team missionary school, international school or boarding school? Pray for MK transitions, especially the transition back to America that often occurs after graduation from high school and at the time of entering university or college. Since mom and dad and children will then be living in different countries, often different continents, frequently separated by an ocean, the sense of separation for both parents and child can be acute. This a critical time for the missionary parents of missionary kids. Missionaries sometimes make the decision to return to the States more or less permanently at this point, again at just the time in their missionary careers when they are becoming the most useful.

4. Spiritual Life

In a pioneer church-planting situation missionaries may have no church available to them. In most church planting situations, if there is a church, it will be small, weak and immature. There will be little or nothing available as a ministry to their children or youth. If they are new missionaries, even if there is an indigenous church, because it will be some time before they are proficient in the language, they will receive little from the church services. Most missionaries are not able to depend on their home church in the States to provide sermon tapes and other materials. Missionaries can also experience a sense of isolation from the Christian world in the West. For example, they will not know what the best Christian books of the last four or five years are since they have been on the field. Missionaries, more than other Christians in the States, must take a very high level of personal responsibility for their spiritual growth and health.

Pray that your missionaries will have a strong personal assurance of salvation, grounded in Christ alone, grace alone, faith alone and the gospel alone. Doubt paralyzes; assurance liberates. Only those who are secure in Christ and know it are free to give themselves away for others. Pray also for their personal and family worship, that they may joyfully and profitably study the Bible and pray, as well as engage in other acts of worship such as singing hymns and Christian songs. John Piper in his book, *Let the Nations Be Glad*, truly said, "You cannot commend what you do not cherish." This means our missionaries must have a vital, growing and deep experience of God if they are to lead others into relationship with Him.

5. Team Relationships

Missionaries are strong willed, independent, with strong ideas about what needs to be done and how it needs to be done. Just to survive on the field requires strong people. When you put a group of people like this on the same team and ask them to work harmoniously together that can be a very tall order indeed. If a team is international in its make up – people speak different native languages, they have different cultural values, as well as other differences – the problems are increased. In fact, failure to get along with each other can be a very serious problem in mission teams and can even result in recall of a missionary. .

Yet Christ-like team relationships are extremely important to effective mission work. We cannot separate the Great Commission from the Great Commandment. A mission team is a miniature church, a model church, which people are watching in order to see something supernatural, to see something of Christ, to confirm and validate the supernatural gospel which the team preaches. What the world needs to see in the life of the team is supernatural love in the team's interpersonal relationships in order to know that these are Christ's true disciples. Pray for humility, flexibility and teachableness for your missionaries.

Pray also that this Christlikeness in relationship may extend to indigenous Christians and to relationships with the home office. As you pray, you may read and reflect upon John 13:34,35; Philippians 2:1-11; I John 4:7-21.

6. Friendships

When we ask our missionaries on the field for specific prayer requests, we are often told, particularly by the women, that they would like us to pray that God would give them one good friend. Sometimes missionaries go to the field with the expectation that another member of the team is going to be a best friend, but this often does not happen. Missionaries leave family, friends and church behind and missionary life can be lonely. This loneliness can be especially severe at holidays and other times when they normally gather with family or friends.

7. Cultural Adjustment, Language Learning and Ministerial Competency

This is an important area for prayer especially for the new, first term missionary, but even the veteran missionary will always need to become more proficient in the language and more at home in the culture.

Most new missionaries have to deal with culture shock as they adjust to their new, strange and perhaps even somewhat frightening adopted culture. Literally everything is new and seems out of control, e.g. new language, customs, different values, a different world and life view and even the aspects of everyday life which we take for granted in our home culture, such as shopping, banking, buying gasoline (or it may be called petrol), renting a house, getting the car repaired, hiring and supervising house and garden help, schooling for the children, and the list goes on seemingly without end, are not only different, but often incomprehensible and sometimes just seem wrong or stupid. This produces stress that results in culture shock. Eventually culture shock goes away as the vast majority of missionaries successfully adjust to the culture. There is something else which can last much longer that I have seen even in veteran missionaries who have been on the field for three or four terms, and I would call it culture fatigue. It is a weariness produced by those cultures which are so different from our own, e.g. in their view of women, as in the Muslim world, or in which business and government are so bureaucratic as to be nearly incomprehensible, and great stress is produced whenever one has to deal with such entities. This kind of cultural fatigue may always exist to some degree and missionaries must find ways to successfully deal with it and adapt to it.

Acquiring language competency is absolutely essential to effective ministry. This competency will take many years in some languages. . Some cultures are very unforgiving concerning the slaughter of their mother tongue by foreigners, while others praise every sincere effort to speak their language though laced with mistakes. Missionaries have differing abilities and aptitude for language learning. Some will do well; others will struggle their entire missionary career. . Language learning must go beyond the ability to converse about the weather or children and the other things of ordinary life. It must include the ability to present and discuss religious and philosophical ideas, such as God, sin, grace, substitutionary atonement, salvation and many other Biblical topics in a way that is understandable and makes sense in the culture.

Language learning can be arduous and discouraging, so pray that the Lord will provide perseverance for this effort. But the effort is worth it, because nothing shows a greater compliment to a culture than to effectively learn the language and to love one's adopted culture. Both of these are keys to effectiveness and longevity in missionary service.

8. Victorious Spiritual Warfare

The gospel is that the Lord Jesus defeated the devil and the spiritual forces of evil at the cross, and not only defeated them, but publicly humiliated them as well, Colossians 2:15. In fact most of Colossians one and two speaks of the superiority of Christ, his deity and his power that are available for the Great Commission. Pray that your missionaries may by faith live and work daily in the reality of this victory of Jesus, especially when their labors for the Lord are painfully slow and seem to be producing very scant fruit. Pray that they will claim Christ's victory and by faith will believe that he possesses universal authority, Matthew 28:18, that he has been raised and exalted to the right hand of the Father far above all rule, authority, power, dominion and title and that the power that raised Christ is still at the disposal of the church and at work in the world for the accomplishment of God's eternal saving purposes(Ephesians 1:19-23).

Pray that your missionaries will not make the mistake of thinking that Satan is a virtual god, nearly equal to Christ. Pray that they will see how puny Satan is in comparison to the Incomparable One, Jesus Christ.

9. Opportunities for the gospel

Pray for conversions, for opportunities to disciple new converts and to plant churches. Pray that your missionaries would be protected from discouragement and depression when results are slow and small and that they would be joyfully faithful to their calling, optimistic believing the promises of God and persevering even when, especially when, progress is minimal.

Some parts of the world are extremely secular and disdain the gospel, e. g. parts of Western Europe. In France, on average, it is said that it takes seventeen years to plant one church, and that church will not be very large by American standards. In the Muslim world of the Middle East and North Africa there can be great hostility to Christians and the Church, especially toward those indigenous Christians who are bold enough to evangelize countrymen.. To become a Christian in such cultures is to invite persecution and even risk one's life. The price for following Christ may literally cost a disciple everything, including life itself. Christian workers who live in these places will find the lack of response and even frequent defections of professing converts to be very discouraging indeed. Some have worked for decades and seen only a handful of people come to faith in Christ. Even in places like Africa and South America where Christianity has been for well over a century , often the church is worldly, legalistic and shallow or it is a paganized, syncretized Christianity, which little resembles true Christian faith. These are only a few examples, but they illustrate how difficult and discouraging missionary life can be, so we need to pray for encouragement for our people on the field.

10. The National Church

Pray for the training of strong, male, indigenous leadership for the church and for the willing transfer of leadership at the appropriate time from the missionaries to the national believers (indigenization). In such a process, pray that the missionaries will have a willingness to accept significant change. As paradigms for mission work change, e. g. as a missionary may move from being the front line church planter to being a trainer, facilitator for the national worker to be the front line church planter, missionaries have to make changes for which they do not always feel well equipped. They may not be as happy with their new role or they may wonder what they are supposed to be doing. If the change is significant enough, they may even have questions about staying with their mission or in mission work at all. Pray that missionaries will be adaptable and willing to accept change because the likelihood is that they will have to do so several times during their missionary careers. Pray also for the formation of strong equal partnerships among the missionaries, the indigenous chuch and the sending churches.

11. Willingness to Suffer

Suffering for Christ is not only the cost of discipleship, but suffering is the means of advancing the gospel. Genuineness of faith is not seen in thanking God for the temporal blessings He gives. Anyone can do that, but in joyfully thanking God when he deprives us of temporal blessings and gives only Himself. Suffering provides a most powerful opportunity for witness. Pray that our missionaries may have a willingness to suffer and endure hardship.

12. More Laborers for the Ripe Harvest Fields

The Biblical strategy for recruitment is prayer (Matthew 9: 35-38).

How to Pray for Chaplains

Chaplain (COL) David Peterson, U.S. Army, Ret.
Coordinator for Chaplain Ministries
Mission to North America

As this book goes to press, the United States is entering a war on terrorism. Our military is on the highest alert, reserves are being called to active service, and many men are enlisting. This is a strategic time for Chaplains in the military. Col. David Peterson, U. S. Army Retired and Coordinator for Chaplain Ministries with Mission to North America, Presbyterian Church in America, prepared the following prayer guide. You are encouraged to use this guide to pray for specific chaplains.

1. Physical well-being of chaplains and their families

Usually chaplains and their families receive excellent medical care; their living conditions are very good wherever they are stationed. But when they are involved in a humanitarian operation, such as Kosovo, Bosnia or comparable missions, we should pray for their safety. And, of course, their safety is a major issue when they go to war or are involved in a military conflict.

2. Marriage and Family Life

Chaplains are away from their families a significant amount of time. Even when they are not on a "separation tour", such as Korea, humanitarian missions, and extended training periods in Europe, they are often "in the field" for extended periods.

The Chaplain's spouse has significant demands placed upon her. Because of the Chaplain's extended absence, she has most of the responsibility for rearing the children, providing religious education, overseeing the secular education, all the while, fulfilling the military and social obligations.

Pornography is more prevalent among the military than in most other situations. Pray that your Chaplain will have a commitment to a regular day off, that they will take their yearly vacation time and that husbands and wives will spend much of this time together on a regular basis to nurture their relationship. Pray for quality and quantity time together for husband and wife. A wife can sometimes feel neglected. Chaplains sometimes forget about their wives and children and their needs. The wife on the other hand may be "stuck at home" with the kids, not as involved in ministry and meeting others.

Aging and infirmed parents may catch military chaplains between two competing and equally important responsibilities: God's call on their lives and God's command to take care of their parents. Pray for the ability to see things clearly and for wisdom from the Lord in this matter of parental care.

3. For CKs (chaplain's kids)

Pray with the children's schooling. It is often a problem because the children are bounced around to many various schools. Consequently, it is difficult for them to develop friendship. In most cases, parents need to accept additional responsibility for their kid's religious education.

4. Spiritual Life

The chaplain's spiritual life is his greatest need. Chaplains work in a very secular society. Fellowship with like-minded Christians is very limited. In most cases, they work in a "macho-type" society. Consequently, individualism and hard living are a high priority. Prayer for the chaplains devotional life, study time, home life is a high priority. Ask the Lord to make the chaplains appropriately courageous in their witness, both verbal and non-verbal. Pray that your Chaplain will not compromise.

5. Team Relationships

Chaplains minister in a pluralistic environment. Consequently, there are quite often unique pressures to be a "Team-Player", in the worst sense of that phrase. On occasion there are subtle and sometimes not so subtle pressures on the evangelical chaplains, to compromise the basic doctrine of the gospel. In fact, the pressures are increasing.

Pray that God will provide meaningful fellowship for both your chaplain and each member of his family. Ask the Lord to grant courage to be faithful to the Gospel in his preaching and counseling. Pray that God will grant appropriate flexibility and teachableness. Ask the Lord to keep your chaplain humble and prevent him from getting caught up in Careerism.

6. Friendships

Pray that God will give one good friend, especially to the Chaplain's wife. Chaplains leave family, friends and church behind and their life can be lonely. This loneliness can be especially severe at holidays and other times when they normally gather with family or friends.

7. Cultural Adjustment, Language Learning and Ministerial Competency

Military chaplains are involved in a unique sub-culture. Chaplain must learn how to work efficiently within the "system." In the military, his credibility is dependent upon professionalism as a service member; he must be physically fit, able to run four miles several times a week. He must train with the troops and live like the troops live.

8. Victorious Spiritual Warfare

"We will never know what prayer is for until we learn that life is war." John Piper, *Let the Nations be Glad.* Military warfare is similar to spiritual militancy but they are not the same (See *Improve Your Prayer Life* p. 46.). Pray that your chaplain will live and work by faith live in the reality of Christ's victory.

9. Opportunities for the gospel

Chaplains have unlimited opportunities to communicate the Gospel to the service members and their families. Individual counseling is continual. In addition chaplains teach Bible studies and preach at worship services. One of the most important things you can pray for your chaplain is that God will keep him faithful to his calling. Chaplains are often asked to share a worship service with very liberal chaplains. When this occasion arises, it is important for the chaplain to boldly proclaim the Gospel in love without unnecessary offense.

Chaplains minister in a community composed of numerous religions and faiths. When assigned to a unit they are considered its pastor. However, the community in most cases is made up of all religions (Muslim, Jewish, Roman Catholic, all types of Protestants, Non-Trinitarians, and those who claim no faith). This presents many challenges, yet many opportunities to present the Gospel.

10. Willingness to Suffer

Except in combat situations, chaplains do not usually experience physical suffering. Their living conditions are normally good. However, chaplains and their families do experience significant hardships in the area of adjustment to new units and locations, separation tours, working in a very secular society, pressures of pluralism, physical demands, and lack of fellowship with like-minded Christians.

11. More Laborers for the Ripe Harvest Fields

Ask the Lord of the Harvest to send forth His laborers into Captaincies.

If your local church has not adopted a chaplain, prayerfully consider this now. Chaplain Ministries seek to interface both with local churches and individual members.

1. Sponsor Churches commit to supporting the chaplain and his family in prayer. Chaplains keep Sponsor Churches informed through a quarterly up-date on his ministry and specific prayer requests. We are asking the Lord to provide three Sponsor Churches for each chaplain.

2. Individual Sponsors: Individual Sponsors pray for a specific chaplain and the chaplain keep Individual Sponsors informed. We are asking the Lord for 120 Individual Sponsors for each chaplain.

The *Guardian* is a quarterly prayer calendar that is mailed to Sponsor Churches and Individuals. For further information on the Adopt a Chaplain ministry, contact Chaplain (COL) David P. Peterson, USA, Ret., at either 21115 Brimstone Place; Sturgis, SD 57785 or dpeterson@pcanet.org.

SELECTED BIBLIOGRAPHY

Jesus, the Model for Prayer

Cushman, Ralph S., *The Prayers of Jesus,* Abingdon, Nashville, TN, 1956. Primarily deals with the High Priestly Prayer of Christ in John 17.

Griffiths, Michael, "The Example of Jesus in Prayer," in *The Example of Jesus,* InterVarsity, Downers Grove, IL, 1985, pp. 159-174,.

Plumber, Alfred "Prayer," Hastings, James, *Dictionary of Christ and the Gospels*, New York: Charles Scribner's Sons, 1908, p. 390-303.

Jeremias, Joachim, *The Prayers of Jesus,* Fortress Press, Philadelphia, PA, 1967, 124 pages.

Lockyer, Herbert, "Prayers and Prayer in the New Testament," *All the Prayers of the Bible*, Grand Rapids, MI, U.S.A.: Zondervan Publishing House, 1973, pp. 173-189.

M'Intry, David M. *The Prayer Life of Our Lord,* Morgan & Scott Ltd. London, n.d.

Murray, Andrew, *With Christ in the School of Prayer, Thoughts on Our Training for the Ministry of Intercession*, Revell, Old Tappan, NJ, 1953, 249 pages.

Sanders, J. Oswald, "The Prayer Life of Christ," Chapter 19, *Prayer Power Unlimited*, Moody Press, Chicago, IL, n.d., pp., 132-137.

Stalker, James, "Christ As A Man of Prayer," pages 126-144, *Imago Christi: The Example of Jesus Christ,* American Tract Society, New York, NY, 1889.

Thomson, James G. C. C., *The Praying Christ,* Eerdman's, Grand Rapids, MI, 1959.

Trueblood, Elton, *The Prayers of Christ*, Prinit Press, Dublin, Indiana, 1981, First published under the title of *The Lord's Prayers,* 1965, 126 pages.

Ministry

Green, Michael, *Called to Serve--Ministry and Ministers in the Church,* Christian Foundations, Volume One. Westminster Press. 1964, Philadelphia, PA. .

Lindsay, Thomas M. *The Church and the Ministry in the Early Centuries*, Hodder and Stoughton, London, 1902.

Manson, T.W. *The Church's Ministry*, Hodder and Stoughton, London England, n.d.

Minchin, G., *Every Man and his Ministry*, *Worship in the Body of Christ,* London: Darton, Longman & Todd, 1960, 1960.

Neill, Stephen, ed., *The Ministry of the Church*, The Canterbury Press, London, 1947.

Swete, H.B., ed., *The Early History of the Church and* ministry, Macmillan, London, 1918.

Torrance, T.F., *Royal Priesthood*, S.J.T. Occasional Papers, Edinburgh: Oliver and Boyd, Ltd. 1963,

.

The Decline of the American Culture

Bennett, William J., *The Death of Courage, Bill Clinton and the Assault on American Ideals,* The Free Press, New York, NY., 1998.

Bloom, Allan, *The Closing of the American Mind, How Higher Education has Failed Democracy and Impoverished the Souls of Today's Students,* Simon Schuster, New York, NY, 1987.

Bork, Robert H., *Slouching Towards Gomorrah, Modern Liberalism and American Decline,* HarperCollins Books, New York, NY, 1996.

Brown, Harold O. J., *The Sensate Culture, Western Civilization between Chaos and Transformation,* Word Publishing, Dallas, TX, 1996.
Colson, Charles, *Against the Night, Living in the New Dark Ages,* Servant Publications, Ann Arbor, MI, 1989.
Colson, Charles, and Jack Eckerd, *Why America Doesn't Work, How the Decline of the Work Ethic is Hurting Your Family and Future—and What You Can Do, Word*, Dallas, TX, 1991.
Cross, Martin L., *The End of Sanity, Social and Cultural Madness in America,* Avon, New York, 1997.
Kelley, Dean, *Why Conservative Churches are Growing, A Study in Sociology of Religion,* Harper & Row, Publishers, San Francisco, 1972.
Kilpatrick, William, *Why Johnny Can't Tell Right from Wrong, Moral Illiteracy and the Case for Character Education,* Simon & Schuster, New York, NY, 1992.
Lasch, Christopher, *The Culture of Narcissism, American Life in an Age of Diminishing Expectations,* W. W. Norton & Company, New York, NY, 1978.
Postman, Neil, *Amusing Ourselves to Death, Public Discourse in the Age of Show Business,* Penguin, New York, NY, 1985.
Ruggiero, Vincent Ryan, *Warning, Nonsense is Destroying America, The Role of Popular Culture in America's Social Problems,* Thomas Nelson Publishers, Nashville, TN, 1994.
Sykes, Charles J., *A Nation of Victims, The Decay of the American Character,* St. Martin Press, New York, NY, 1992.

Work is Ministry

Peabody, Larry, *Secular Work is Full-Time Service,* Christian Literature Crusade, Fort Washington, PA, 1974.

The Word in Life Study Bible, Discover the Truths of God's Word for You and Your World, New Testament Edition, Nelson, Nashville, TN, 1993. "A Glance at Work in the Bible," p. 929, "Jobs and Occupation Index," pp. 971-1013.

The Antichristian Spirit of Today

Carter, Stephen L., *Culture of Disbelief, How American Law and Politics Trivialize Religious Devotion*, Basicbooks, NY, 1993. 328pp. Index. Explains how we can preserve the vital separation of church and state while embracing rather than trivializing the faith of millions.
Carter, Stephen L., *God's Name in Vain: The Wrongs and Rights of Religion in Politics*, NY Basic Books 2000.
Lapin, Daniel, *America's Real War, An Orthodox Rabbi Insists that Judeo-Christian Values are Vital for Our Nation's Survival,* Multinomah Publishers, Sisters, OR, 1999. Rabbi Lapin says, "If the term "anti-semitism" is to retain any intellectual and moral integrity, we must also today admit to the term "anti-Christian." p. 39. And, "We are no longer one nation under God. We are two separate nations with two distinct and incompatible moral visions." p. 45.

The Church--Negative

Barna, George, *Marketing the Church, What They Never Taught You About Church Growth,* NAVPRESS, Colorado Springs, CO, 1988.
Barna, George, *The Second Coming of the Church, A Blueprint for Survival,* Word Publishing, Nashville, TN, 1998.
Barna, George and Mark Hatch, *Boiling Point, It only Takes One Degree, Monitoring Cultural Shifts in the 21st Century,* Regal Books, Ventura, CA, 2001.

Bloesch, Donald G., *The Crisis of Piety, Essays Toward a Theology of the Christian Life,* Eerdmans, Grand Rapids, MI, 1968.

Clapp, Rodney, *A Peculiar People, The Church as Culture in a Post-Christian Society,* Downers Grove, IL. 1995.

Dawn, Marva, *Reaching out with Dumbing Down,* Grand Rapids, MI: William B. Eerdmans Publishing Co., Grand Rapids, 1995

Ellul, Jacques, *The Subversion of Christianity,* Eerdman, Grand Rapids, MI, 1986.

Guinness, Os, *The Call, Find and Fulfilling the Central Purpose for Your Life,* Word Publishing, Nashville, TN, 1998.

Guinness, Os, *The Gravedigger File, Papers on the Subversion of the Modern Church,* Inter-Varsity Press, Downers Grove, IL, 1983.

Guinness, Os, *Unbridling Our Times, Reflections on the Gathering Cultural Crisis,* Baker Books, Grand Rapids, MI, 1999.

Hendricks, William D., *Exit Interviews, Revealing Stories of Why People are Leaving the Church,* Moody, Chicago, IL, 1993.

Lewis, C. S., *The Weight of Glory, and Other Addresses,* Macmillian, New York, 1980.

MacArthur, Jr., John F., *Ashamed of the Gospel, When the Church becomes Like the World,* Crossway Books, Wheaton, IL, 1993.

Muggeridge, Malcolm, *The End of Christendom,* Eerdmans, Grand Rapids, MI, 1980.

Podles, Leon, J., *The Church Impotent, The Feminization of Christianity,* Spence Publishing, Dallas, TX, 1999.

Wells, *No Place for Truth, Or Whatever Happened to Evangelical Theology,* Eerdmans, Grand Rapids, MI, 1993.

Peterson, Jim, *Church Without Walls, Moving Beyond Traditional Boundaries,* NavPress, Colorado Springs, CO 1992.

Snyder, Howard A. *Liberating the Church, the Ecology of Church & Kingdom,* Inter-Varsity Press, Downers Grove, IL, 1983.

Snyder, Howard A. *The Problem of Wine Skins, Church Structure in a Technological Age,* Inter-Varsity Press, Downers Grove, IL, 1978.

Snyder, Howard A. *The Community of the King,* Inter-Varsity Press, Downers Grove, IL, 1975.

Wells, David, *God in the Wasteland, The Reality of Truth in a World of Fading Dreams,* Eerdmans, Grand Rapids, MI, 1994.

The Church--Positive

Alexander, Donald L., *Christian Spirituality, Five Views of Sanctification,* Inter-Varsity, Downer's Grove, IL, 1988.

Allen, Roland, *Missionary Methods, St. Paul's or Ours?* Eerdmans, Grand Rapids, MI, 1962.

Allen, Roland, *The Ministry of the Spirit, Selected Writings,* Eerdmans, Grand Rapids, MI, 1960.

Avis, Paul D. L., *The Church in the Theology of the Reformers*, Atlanta, John Knox, 1981.

Banks, Robert, *Paul's Idea of Community: The Early House Churches in Their Historical Setting, Eerdmans,* Grand Rapids, MI, 1980.

Bannerman, James, *The Church of Christ, A Treatise on the Nature, powers, ordinances, discipline and Government of the Christian Church, 2 volumes,* The Banner of Truth Trust, Edinburgh, First published 1869, reprint 1974.

Berkouwer, G. C., *Studies in Dogmatics, The Church*, Eerdmans, Grand Rapids, MI, 1976.

Blau, Johannes, *The Missionary Nature of the Church,* McGraw-Hill, New York, 1962.
Buhlmann, Walbert, *Courage Church, Essays in Ecclesial Spirituality,* Orbis Books, Maryknoll, New York, 1978.
Buhlmann, Walbert, *The Coming of the Third Church, an Analysis of the Present and the Future Church,* Orbis Books, Maryknoll, New York, 1978.
Callahan, Kennon L., *Effective Church Leadership: Building on the Twelve Keys,* San Francisco, CA, Harper & Row, 1990.
Guder, Darrell L., *Missional Church, A Vision for the Sending of the Church in the North America,* Eerdmans, Grand Rapids, 1998.
Kraemer, Hendrik, *A Theology of the Laity,* Westminster Press, Philadelphia, PA. 1958.
Kung, Hans, *The Church,* Search Press, London, 1973.
Leivestad, R. *Christ the Conqueror--Ideas of Conflict and Victory in the New Testament*, SPCK, London, 1954.
Llyod-Jones, D. Martyn, *The Basis of Christian Unity,* Eerdmans, Grand Rapids, MI, 1962.
Minear, Paul S. *Horizons of Christian Community,* St. Louis, MO: Bethany Press, 1959.
Minear, Paul S. *Images of the Church in the New Testament,* Westminster Press, Philadelphia, PA, 1960.
Minear, Paul S., *Jesus and His People—World Christian Books, No. 11,* Lutterworth, 1957.
Minear, Paul S. *The Kingdom and the Power, an Exposition of the New Testament Gospel,* Westminster Press, 1960.
Minear, Paul S., *The Nature of the Unity We Seek,* Bethany Press, St. Louis, MO, 1958.
Minear, Paul S. *To Die and to Live: Christ's Resurrection and Christians Vocation,* Seabury, NY 1977.
Moltmann, Jurgen, *The Church in the Power of the Spirit,* Harper and Row, New York, NY, 1975.

Morris, Leon, *Minister of God,* Inter-Varsity Press, Downers Grove, IL, 1973.

Owen, John, *The True Nature of a Gospel Church and Its Government (1689),* James Clarke & Co. London, 1947.

Schaeffer, Francis, A., *True Spirituality,* Tyndale House, Wheaton, IL, 1972.

Schmidt, Karl Ludwig, *The Church, Bible Key Words from Gerhard Kittle's Theologisches Worterbuch Zum Neuen Testament,* Adam and Charles Black, London, 1950.

Stott, John R. W., *Evangelical Truth, A Personal Plea for Unity, Integrity & Faithfulness,* Inter-Varsity Press, Downers Grove, IL, 1999.

Stott, John R. W., *One People, Clergy and Laity in God's Church,* Falcon Books, London, 1969.

Stott, John R. W., *What Christ Thinks of the Church, Expository addresses on the first three chapters of the Book of Revelation,* Eerdmans, Grand Rapids, 1958.

Trueblood, Elton, *The Company of the Committed, A Bold and Imaginative Re-thinking of the Strategy of the Church in Contemporary Life,* Harper & Row, New York, NY, 1961.

Trueblood, Elton, *The Incendiary Fellowship,* Harper & Row, New York, NY, 1967.

Charles Van Engen, *God's Missionary People, Rethinking the Purpose of the Local Church,* Baker Book House, Grand Rapids, MI, 1991.

Leadership

Burns, James MacGregor, *Leadership,* Harper & Row Publishers, New York, NY, 1978.

DePree, Max, *Leadership is an Art,* Doubleday, New York, NY, 1989.

Pastors

Barna, George, *The Frog in the Kettle, What Christians Need to Know about Life in the Year 2000,* Regal Books, Ventura, CA, 1990.

Barna, George, *Today's Pastors, A Revealing Look at What Pastors are saying about Themselves their Peers and the Pressures they Face,* Regal Books, Ventura, CA, 1993.

Baxter, Richard, *The Reformed Pastor,* National Foundation for Christian Education, Marshalton, DE, n.d.

McBurney, *Every Pastor Needs a Pastor,* Pastoral Ministry Resources, Carbondale, CO, 1977.

Roberts, Wes, *Support Your Local Pastor, Practical Ways to Encourage Your Minister,* NavPress, Colorado Springs, CO, 1995.

Rediger, G. Lloyd, *Clergy Killers, Guide for Pastors and Congregations Under Attack,* Westminster-John Knox Press, Louisville, KY, 1997.

Biography of Prayer Warriors

Grubb, Norman, *Reese Howell, Intercessor,* Christian Literature Crusade, Fort Washington, PA, 1952.

Miller, Basil, *George Muller, The Man of Faith,* Zondervan, Grand Rapids, MI, 1941.

Pierson, Authur T., *George Muller of Bristol and His Witness to a Prayer-Hearing God,* Loizeaux Brothers, New York, NY, 1899.

Reid, W. Stanford, *Trumpeter of God,* Charles Scribner's Sons, New York, 1974. The biography of John Knox.

Multiethnic Ministry

Emerson, Michael O. and Christian Smith, *Divided by Faith*, Oxford University Press, 2000.

Greely, Andrew M. *Why Can't They Be Like Us?* New York: D. P. Dutton, 1975.

Ortiz, Manuel *The Hispanic Challenge: Opportunities Confronting the Church,* Downers Grove: Inter-Varsity Press, 1993.

Ortiz, Manuel *One New People: Models for Developing a Multiethnic Church,* Downers Grove: Inter-Varsity Press, 1996.

Romo, Oscar I. *American Mosaic: Church Planting in Ethnic America,* Nashville: Broadman Press, 1993.

Dear Kingdom Intercessor,

Jesus commanded, "Watch and pray" (Matthew 26:41). Here at SERVE we take this command very seriously. The American culture is collapsing because the majority of the churches in this land are powerless as a consequence of their prayerlessness. God directed us in the development of the Kingdom Campaign to correct this deficiency. The Kingdom Campaign Vision is to equip 120 kingdom Intercessors in 120 churches in 120 cities. We have trained leaders from coast to coast. Listen to what just a few of them are saying.

> "Kingdom Campaign Leadership Training provided motivation, structure, and direction for improving my personal and corporate prayer life."

> "It (Kingdom Intercessor Training) helped me to fully realize both the power of prayer and how to pray more effectively."

> "The training gave me practical steps to follow in praying. It encouraged me to be obedient, active, and expectant in respect to the answers to my prayers. Many encouraging examples were told of how God has worked through prayer."

SERVE International is a non-profit 501c3 ministry committed to equipping Christians to pray more biblically. SERVE ministers to a wide range of evangelical churches of varying sizes whose leaders are eager to be part of this growing movement. SERVE is funded by gifts from those who share our heart for the kingdom.

Will you prayerfully consider investing in the Lord's work through SERVE? You may send your gift to SERVE International, Inc., 4646 N. Shallowford Road, Suite 200, Atlanta, GA 30338. You may want to add a gift amount to your purchase of materials on page 279.

Thank you for your prayerful consideration.

Archie Parrish, President
SERVE International, Inc.

Improve Your Prayer Life
$7.00

How to transform instinctive, reactive prayer into biblical, proactive, kingdom-focused prayer

John Piper says, "You will never know what prayer is for, until you learn that life is war." Your eyes will be opened to the reality of the war that Christians are in today. Military battles in the Bible show you how to strategically fight against the enemy with your super-weapon—kingdom-focused prayer. Basic training is provided to get you in shape to be an effective prayer warrior.

Use this book as the first training manual in the Kingdom Campaign series to help you establish the discipline of praying with a kingdom focus for 15 minute daily.

Intercede For and With Your Family $7.00

How to achieve God's purpose for your family through kingdom-focused prayer

If you want the blessing of heaven upon your family, if you want your children to make their future homes "houses of prayer," if you want the Christian faith to thrive from age to age, then begin and continue the worship of God with your family. Learn God's purpose and order for the family and how to pray together.

This second book in the series helps you add to your daily discipline 15 minutes of prayer for and with your family—totaling 30 minutes of kingdom-focused prayer.

Invigorate Your Church
$7.00

How to pray with kingdom focus for the leaders and workers of your church so that it becomes all God desires it to be

Without prayer, leaders become prey for the world, the flesh, and the devil. Pastors need members' prayer to be the godly leaders they must be. And, in many churches, 20% of the members do 100% of the work; they are burning out! The remaining 80% are rusting out! Learn how to lift up your pastors, leaders, and laborers.

This third book in the Kingdom Campaign series helps you add another 15 minutes of daily prayer focused on your church—a total of 45 minutes daily.

Impact Your World $7.00

How to pray with kingdom focus so that your family. friends, associates and neighbors are gripped with the gospel

It is no accident that you have relationships with unbelievers—those who are not gripped with the gospel. Learn the Who, What, When, Why, and How of praying for the ungripped so you can effectively reach them for Christ. This really equips and motivates you to share your faith!

This fourth book in the series helps you add 15 minutes of prayer for your lost world to your daily discipline—a total of 1 hour a day of kingdom-focused prayer.

Ignite Your Leadership
$7.00

How to implement the chain of encouragement to help the Church build and use its super weapon—kingdom-focused prayer

The present plight of the church demands that Christians stand our ground and not give another inch to the enemy! We are at war—spiritual war—and the greatest need in the world today is leaders. Find out how to build a chain of encouragement of 120 kingdom intercessors.

This guide for fireteam leaders provides insight and specific instructions for directing your group through all four stages of the Kingdom Campaign using the other books listed.

Prices for publications are subject to change without notice.

For credit card orders, please:
Fax: (770) 682-4979
or e-mail: info@kingdomprayer.org
Or, mail order with payment to:

4646 N. Shallowford Road
Suite 200
Atlanta, GA 30338

For bulk orders, please:
Fax: (770) 682-4979
or e-mail: info@kingdomprayer.org

All international orders must be paid for by credit card

Name ______________________________

Street Address ______________________________
(Materials cannot be delivered to a PO box)

City, State, ZIP ______________________________

Phone ______________________________

E-mail Address ______________________________

Title	Qty.	Total
Improve Your Prayer Life		$
Intercede For and With Your Family		
Invigorate Your Church		
Impact Your World		
Ignite Your Leadership		
	Subtotal (carry this amount to next page)	$

(Order form continued). . .

Subtotal (from previous page)	$
GA residents add 7.00% sales tax	$
Shipping (see table below)	$
*Donation to SERVE International, Inc.	$
TOTAL ENCLOSED (US FUNDS ONLY)	$

Standard Shipping Rate Table for US only

Amount of Subtotal	**Add**
$20.00 and under	$3.00
$20.01- $50.00	$6.00
$50.01 - $100.00	$10.00
Over $100.00	10% of amount of order

Please allow 20 days for delivery.

For international orders, please call, fax, or email your order with credit card number and expiration date. The actual shipping costs will be added to your billing. Allow 6 weeks for delivery.

METHOD OF PAYMENT:

☐ Check/Money Order
(please make payable to SERVE International, Inc.)

☐ Credit Card - Circle one: VISA Master Card

Credit Card No.:______________________________

Exp. Date: ______________________________

Signature: ______________________________

*SERVE International, Inc. is a non-profit organization that relies primarily on tax-deductible gifts to fund its operations.

(Permission granted to photocopy pages 277 and 278)